Executive Advantage

Executive Advantage

Resilient leadership for 21st-century organizations

Dr Jacqui Grey

KoganPage

LONDON PHILADELPHIA NEW DELHI

First published in Great Britain and the United States in 2013 by Kogan Page Limited

2nd Floor, 45 Gee Street	1518 Walnut Street, Suite 1100	4737/23 Ansari Road
London EC1V 3RS	Philadelphia PA 19102	Daryaganj
United Kingdom	USA	New Delhi 110002
www.koganpage.com		India

© Jacqui Grey, 2013

The right of Jacqui Grey to be identified as the author of this work has been asserted by her in accordance with the Copyright, Designs and Patents Act 1988.

ISBN   978 0 7494 6828 6
E-ISBN   978 0 7494 6829 3

British Library Cataloguing-in-Publication Data

A CIP record for this book is available from the British Library.

Library of Congress Cataloging-in-Publication Data

Grey, Jacqui.
    Executive advantage : resilient leadership for 21st-century organizations / Jacqui Grey.
        p. cm.
    Includes bibliographical references and index.
    ISBN 978-0-7494-6828-6 – ISBN 978-0-7494-6829-3   1. Leadership.   2. Executive ability.
3. Organizational change.   4. Success in business.   I. Title.
    HD57.7.G744 2013
    658.4′092–dc23
                                                                    2012034464

Typeset by Graphicraft Limited, Hong Kong
Printed and bound by CPI Group (UK) Ltd, Croydon, CR0 4YY

CONTENTS

ACKNOWLEDGEMENTS

Many thanks to the people who kindly agreed to be interviewed for this book. They were:

Ansell, Clive – CEO Tribal Technology, Tribal Group plc

Barry, Subha – ex chief diversity officer, Merrill Lynch

Berry, Maggie – MD, womenintechnology.co.uk

Bingham, Liz – managing partner for People and Talent, UK and Ireland, Ernst & Young

Boyle, June – director and head, Scotland YSC

Briault, Fiona – operations director, Central Retail, Asda

Brown, Tim – CEO, Postcomm

Brushfield, Rachel – career coach, Energise Ltd

Cox, Bruce – MD, Diamonds, Rio Tinto

Duberry, Jackie – director HR and corporate services AHDB

Furniss, Jane – CEO, Independent Police Complaints Commission

Lattimor, Andrea – Risk, Compliance and HR director, Intelligent Processing Solutions Ltd (iPSL)

McBain, Mandy – Lieutenant Commander Royal Navy, Naval Service Equality, Diversity and Inclusion Policy

Mendelson, Michelle – EMEA head of diversity and inclusion, Credit Suisse

Merry, Chris – CEO, RSM Tenon

Mills, Eleanor – associate editor, *The Sunday Times*

Mohan, Stephen – MD, Operational Services, Cofunds Limited

Murphy, Vanessa – Diversity and Inclusion Manager, Royal Navy

Murray, Kevin – chairman, The Good Relations Group, part of Chime Communications plc

Phillips, Mark – SVP Medicine and Process Delivery, GSK

Roussouw, Michelle – director in the Board and Advisory Practice, Stonehaven Associates

Shanker, Siva – corporate finance director, SEGRO

Small, Jeremy – group company secretary, Axa UK Ltd

Tucker, Terry – director of learning and organizational development, Barchester Healthcare

Wax, Ruby – TV presenter and leadership communication specialist

Wigley, Bob – chairman, Yell and Stonehaven

Many thanks also to the people who informally gave their views. These include Sarah Churchman, head of diversity at PWC, Linda Pollard OBE, Dr David Rock, CEO at The Neuroleadership Group, Dr Anne Moir, Helen Wells, director of Opportunity Now and Sarah Williams Gardner, government affairs director at IBM UK Ltd. Your time and support are greatly appreciated.

Illustrations by Hadleigh Maunder

BIOGRAPHY

Dr Jacqui Grey FCIPD

A thought leader in Resilience and Authentic 21st-century Leadership, Jacqui has had significant success in helping individuals and companies to achieve amazing results through growth and change. She has participated in mergers, acquisitions, flotation, company sales, takeovers and downsizing. Her background in law, HR at Board level, in FTSE 100 companies (most recently as FVP for EMEA for Merrill Lynch) and success as a small business entrepreneur has created an outstanding toolkit for her work as a top-level business mentor with Merryck & Co. She has a master's degree in Change Management and Strategy and a doctorate in Executive Anxiety, yet her style is not academic but rather business results-focused, pragmatic, flexible and fun.

Jacqui has worked globally for blue-chip companies on innovative Leadership Development programmes and has a special interest in the development of top female executives. She presents at leadership conferences on Authentic 21st-century Leadership, sometimes with

Ruby Wax. She has previously worked for leading investment banks (Merrill Lynch, Credit Suisse, RBS, Barclays, Marks and Spencer Financial Services), IT and telecoms companies (BT, Vodafone, Cisco, Azlan) and more (GSK, Aventis, United Airlines, Burberrys, Allied Milling and Baking and Oxford University Press). She has also guest-presented at business schools including Cranfield, London Business School, IE Business School Madrid and Barchester.

Jacqui has a regular column on leadership in *Pharmacy Management Magazine* and writes regularly for the CEO Forum *Critical Eye* on the subject of getting more executive women on boards. She has been included by invitation in the *Marquis Who's Who in the World*® and is a Fellow of The Chartered Institute of Personnel and Development.

Introduction

Banish Executive Gremlins – become a resilient 21st-century leader

> *Almost £1 billion was wiped off Lloyds's market value after the boss of the state-backed banking group went on immediate sick leave. Shares plummeted after António Horta-Osório began an enforced break barely eight months after taking on one of the biggest jobs in British finance. The Portuguese-born banker, who became chief executive in March 2011 with a package worth around £8.3 million, had been diagnosed with extreme fatigue and stress due to overwork.*
>
> *The unexpected announcement caused turmoil in the part-nationalized bank and sent Lloyds's shares sliding. By the close of trading that night they had dropped by 4.4 per cent, ending the day 1.36p down at 29.2p. That was the biggest percentage fall in the FTSE 500 and wiped £930 million off the value of Lloyds Banking Group. It left the taxpayer, who owns 40 per cent of the bank, £372 million worse off.*

Mail Online 2011

This book illustrates the executive advantage inherent in overcoming the challenges of 21st-century leadership. It introduces human needs (including the need to feel important, powerful, in control and liked) and shows the power and executive advantage that can be obtained in understanding executive anxiety and how, when these needs are not met, they manifest as Executive Gremlins in your business – your own, your board's, your competitors'. It will help you and your organization avoid being derailed by them. Executive anxiety and meeting needs are subjects not often talked about by leaders in organizations so The Executive Advantage 10-Step Solution for Resilient 21st-century Leaders©, which tackles them head on, is the secret weapon in the leader's armoury. It has been developed to build resilience, a key 21st-century leadership capability. The pace and pressures on 21st-century leaders mean they have to be more resilient than ever before. Resilience underpins the ability to be authentic, flexible and inclusive. Before leading others, you must be able to manage yourself.

You picked up this book because you have a need, a desire to be a better leader perhaps, or because you are struggling to handle the day-to-day relentlessness of your job. It could have just been curiosity – you were a bit bored and looking at this book fulfilled a short-term need for mental stimulation while you waited for a train, plane or cappuccino. Or it could have been a more important, deeper need – and something in the title of this book said it might address something bigger or more complex in your life – not necessarily a bad thing.

This book provides a framework for identifying the reasons why leaders get stressed under pressure and strategies for coping with these pressures. It introduces the concept of Executive Gremlins and provides a way for leaders to take stock at *any* moment in time and make better decisions and choices *in the moment*. It helps leaders to model how to handle pressure for younger talent coming through the ranks. It will help leaders to understand how to build an inclusive powerful 21st-century business culture.

Leaders have always had strengths, needs, desires and fears. If needs are met, a strong sense of self and happiness ensues. If not met, they lead to fear and anxiety. The challenge for 21st-century leadership is to be agile, flexible, inclusive and resilient whilst managing our own health and happiness. It also requires us to have effective strategies for when our brains register a threat response and the Executive Gremlins take over. I have seen how Executive Gremlins derail business strategy and I have worked with numerous executives going through painful change. Some of these leaders managed the pressure well, whilst others did not. Personal resilience is key. Most leaders want to feel powerful, popular and in control. These are sometimes aspirations at odds with daily life in the 21st-century organization. We are constantly fighting to make sense of our worlds, to keep on top of things, to not mess up, to meet seemingly impossible deadlines. Our brains overload, making rational thought and personal fulfilment difficult to achieve. Psychological resilience in leaders refers to an individual's ability to cope with stress and emotional pressure. This coping may result in the individual bouncing back after a difficult time, or using the experience of pressure to produce a steeling effect and improved decision-making ability. It proofs us against future stress and makes us stronger. This is sometimes also known as learning from 'crucibles of experience'.

Executive Gremlins may be referred to as 'the little voice in the head' (the one that keeps you awake at night worrying about work the next day), buttons and stress triggers (personal areas of sensitivity that cause us to overreact to a situation), terms that are used interchangeably later in the book. They are the reason leaders derail during times of extreme stress. Executive Gremlins are the tiny things that cause the machine to fail. The machine in this case is both the organization, particularly those going through strategic change (things like mergers and acquisitions or downsizing) *and also* the leader who is trying to make sense of their competing priorities and pressures.

Most successful leaders of businesses today read about and attempt to demonstrate authenticity and emotional intelligence and eventually they become philanthropists with a desire to give something back. However, many of these same leaders fail to *feel* successful under pressure. They acquire the trappings of success, the big cars, the offices and trophies, yet their Executive Gremlins cause them to fear losing control, of being perceived as unimportant or weak, of feeling slighted or unpopular. Executive Gremlins come from the negative fears and perceptions we already have about ourselves. The stress of high-powered jobs exacerbates these negative feelings and may lead to burnout.

CASE STUDY

Many years ago, I observed the CEO of a well-known company sitting in his massive office in his massive chair with his legs curled up in the foetal position rocking – he was that scared. And yes, with the knowledge I had then, I did send for the men in the white jackets. He is fine today but at the time he was paralyzed by the fact that his business was going down and it was 'his fault'. The fact that the parent company that owned his had caused the landslide that was taking his business down meant nothing. He saw it as a huge personal failure. Subsequently, though, he didn't make good decisions and ultimately his company did fail. If I had known then what I know now, and if he had been able to understand what was happening to him, and made different decisions, we might have saved it. We were in board meetings day and night, flying to the USA and renegotiating contracts but we were all *reacting* to our personal fears rather than *responding* to the situation in a more logical way. We were all owed, and lost, a lot of money.

This is an extreme example but every day leaders in organizations make poor decisions because of their fears and anxieties. Understanding them and those of others gives us a significant executive advantage.

21st-century leaders suffer enormous amounts of stress. Much has been written about it – though what is written is often conflicting, confusing and contradictory. The only consensus seems to be in the magnitude of the problem. Philip Burguieres described leaving his $900,000 job because of clinical depression and how he contemplated suicide. Burguieres believes that 'illness is rife among business leaders, and is kept concealed because of stigma' (*The Times*, 2007).

Whilst I do not necessarily agree that most leaders are that far gone, the majority of leaders, whether CEO, department head or team leader in a busy environment, just like most people in general, suffer from some level of internal fear and insecurity, the existence of which they may be totally ignorant of. Stress is exacerbated by executives' own inner worlds, their perceptions, their beliefs and their values.

Neuroscience tells us that the brain tends to see other people as friend or foe but when under stress, tends to the latter. Communication and trust break down and change is resisted.

Executive fears or gremlins are common to all but not the same for each individual. Executives need different solutions to stress because they have different fears, different commercial environments and different external pressures. However, if there is one thing that *is* universal, it is the prevailing tendency to suffer in silence because of the stigma attached to showing weakness and asking for help.

The 21st-century leadership dilemma

FIGURE 0.1

Economists tell us that the key areas for concern for 21st-century leaders working in global businesses today are:

- energy;
- technology;
- geopolitics and population.

Energy is still relatively cheap when produced from fossil fuels. However, the world's remaining oil is produced in unstable, non-democratic countries (like Nigeria, the Middle East, Venezuela and Russia) or hard-to-get-to places (like the deep-sea gulf of Mexico, the Arctic, the Canadian tar sands). Governments are increasing tax on fuels in an attempt to slow climate change (or at least that's what we are told) and renewable, sustainable fuels (like solar power) are still very expensive.

Technology is still moving faster than most of us can keep up with. There are seven key technologies to watch (and just to make things more complicated some of them relate to energy!):

- Renewable energy – like solar power.
- Electric cars – but let's not go into where the electricity comes from …
- Carbon capture – which will mean we may all be using coal again.
- Geo engineering – don't worry about the ozone layer being destroyed; just spray the stratosphere!
- Mobile computing – developing our link to 'clouds'.
- Graphene electronics – making small electronic parts and replacing silicon.
- Personal genomics – we will soon be able to manage our own healthcare.

With regard to geopolitics, in the 19th century the British Empire ruled the world; in the 20th century it was the US empire. In the next century the balance of power is set to shift east. The current world population is set to grow to 10.5 billion by 2050. China's population will grow from 1.3 billion to 1.45 billion and India will stay roughly the same at 1.4 billion. The USA will grow from 304 million to 352 million, Europe will grow from 603 million to 659 million (Russia and the ex-Soviet states will add another 300 million). Asia's growing economic power is translating into greater political and military power and it is entirely possible that this could lead to conflicts between nations as it did in the early 20th century when East and West failed to adjust to each other. China's economy is growing at more than 9 per cent and India's 8 per cent. China is the world's second largest global economy and is set to overtake Japan by 2020. Its GDP is set to overtake the USA's by 2016. China is the centre of global manufacturing, whilst India is dominating IT and outsourcing exports, worth over US$50 billion. AsiaPac now accounts for 38 per cent of the world's economy, with Europe second and the USA third. Sixty-seven per cent of GDP now comes from three countries – China, India and Japan. However, much of the West has more stable political systems than emerging eastern nations and US dominance in global currency markets is enormous – it is very unlikely it will lose that edge in the foreseeable future. Nevertheless, the increasing shift of power from West to East will have huge cultural implications for leaders of organizations. Most leaders in the Western world grew up under a Western model of capitalism. Assumptions are made every day about how we do business. Leaders are judged by largely Western behavioural competencies. Will these be challenged when the USA is no longer the world superpower? I once worked with a huge American airline with offices around the globe, including the Far East. I was running their accredited leadership programme. Running it in the USA was pretty straightforward but this absolutely wasn't the case in Japan and Hawaii where there were big differences in what was considered applicable and appropriate. For instance, one area of contrast lay in the realms of what constituted 'assertive' behaviour in a leader. Japanese women were not able to behave in a way appropriate to the course because of their cultural upbringing and many failed. I was very uncomfortable with this but I did not design the programme, nor have authority to change it. This was stressful for me as I was in the firing line. Leaders will be dealing with these sorts of issues more and more and will be challenged to change their own behaviour, even when the organization may not be changing fast enough to support them. Leaders will need to be flexible. What stresses us will also be different. For example, loss of face is a huge stressor in the East, whereas loss of status may be more important in the West. Leaders must work out how this will affect their own organizations. In addition, as more and more businesses operate globally, executives are expected to be able to operate 24/7 and to travel constantly. Lack of sleep and interrupted sleep patterns are known to impair the brain's ability to function and we lose the ability to think rationally. Add to this the generally unstable position of many Western economies and it becomes clear that the pressure on leaders of governments and organizations is enormous.

I do not claim to be an expert in world economics. However, I am confident that leaders need a new set of 21st-century leadership capabilities to make it through. The economic trends will mean an increase in pace, complexity, change and variety of culture. This will create pressure for the busy executive. The 10-Step Solution for Resilient 21st-century Leaders© and solutions for organizations will give you an executive advantage when dealing with the pressures these changes will inevitably exert.

Having worked with many leaders struggling with these changes, I believe the key behavioural capabilities of being a successful 21st-century leader in an organization today are authentic flexibility and agility, inclusion and resilience. This book's primary focus is resilience. Leaders must learn to be more resilient, to identify their stress *in the moment* and to notice when it happens in others and to take action. By using the Executive Advantage 10-Step Solution, leaders can identify what is going on and make new decisions for the benefit of their organizations. Stress and anxiety can no longer be swept under the carpet. We must recognize that they exist and put in place organizational development programmes and processes that support leaders in developing resilience day to day (I explore organizational solutions more fully in Chapter 8).

The pace of change and increased complexity in organizations, together with globalization, mean leaders must be flexible and adaptable.

FIGURE 0.2

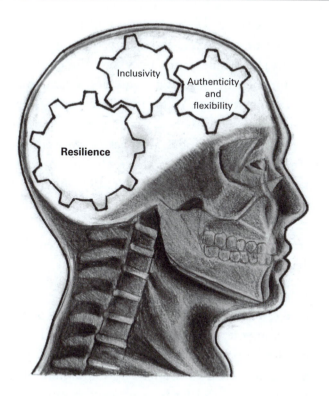

You must be able to adjust your plans in the moment. It is no longer possible to operate 'command and control' structures; leaders must be agile in decision making and empower their people to make decisions according to the needs of the business at the time. You must be able to flex your own style and to utilize different leadership styles according to the situation you find yourself in. However, you must do this authentically, developing ways of flexing your style whilst remaining true to yourself. People will spot a phoney. Someone who is normally fairly dictatorial and controlling will find it very difficult to suddenly become laissez-faire and vice versa! It is no longer possible to pre-empt market changes and global trends in the same way. Leaders must learn to *respond* to market and external conditions rather than *react*.

The massive growth in population and consequent shift of world power mean inclusive leadership is no longer a 'nice to have' but a commercial imperative. Despite increasing unemployment, there is still a shortage of top talent and talent will not come primarily from the West. The Chinese are busy recruiting top professors and lecturers for their brand new universities. Research grants and laboratories are being offered. Young leaders are increasingly mobile, seeking opportunities for growth. Companies cannot afford to over-look or stifle them. This includes all types of diverse groups, from getting more women on boards, to removing barriers around ethnicity, sexuality and disability. It is really down to removing unconscious bias. No rational, intelligent leader is racist or sexist any more, but that doesn't prevent unconscious bias in decision making re hiring and promotion. It is no longer acceptable, or com-mercial, to have only white, middle-aged, middle-class men at the top of global businesses.

The main focus of this book is resilience. The pressures of 21st-century leadership are immense. There is no downtime, markets open and close around the world at different times, shareholder pressure is relentless, the tenure of CEOs is often short and quite often there is a complete turnover of top leaders when companies are merged, acquired or sold. Resilience underpins people's ability to be agile and inclusive. If we are stressed we tend to find it difficult to make deci-sions and we withdraw. In neuroleadership terms, the limbic system takes over from the prefrontal cortex in the brain – and rational thought goes and our animal selves come to the fore.

CASE STUDY

I was on holiday the Monday that Lehman's collapsed and Merrill Lynch did the deal with Bank of America. I started receiving texts from my team at Merrill's at about 7am asking what I knew. I knew nothing! As the details started to unravel, through TV, newspapers and leadership teleconferences with the USA, we filled in the gaps. What became clear was that the CEO of Merrill Lynch had made some great decisions. He saved the bank from total collapse. The terms and details were not all worked out but in principle the deal was done. It was perhaps even more surprising as he must have known that he would lose his job as a result in the coming months. He kept his head and *responded rather than reacted*. He did not allow the pressure he was under, or his ego, to control him, as other leaders were doing elsewhere during the banking crisis (which ultimately led to the collapse of their banks). Many other leaders were controlled by their anxieties and what it might mean for them whereas he remained visible, gave regular briefings and moved on.

We are often more judgemental and suspicious of others who are 'not like us'. Stress that is not owned and dealt with may cause illness and depression and in some extreme cases drive leaders to suicide. The Executive Advantage 10-Step Solution will help.

This book bridges the worlds of organizations, academia and leadership development. It combines my board level corporate experience with my current knowledge and experience as a business mentor/ coach and leadership presenter. It also utilizes research I originally undertook for both for my doctorate and for this book. *Executive Advantage* draws on over 30 case studies from my work as an executive coach and ex-HRD working at board level for over 20 years. I also include findings from interviews with over 30 executives. Case studies were drawn from multinationals, city law firms, investment banks, retail, manufacturing, IT, telecoms, oil companies and more. Their views were remarkably consistent.

Some MBA programmes focus on academic models, compelling speakers, and case studies. Occupational psychologists and therapists don't always have corporate backgrounds or relevant experience to help. Yet in organizations where burnout occurs, leaders are sent for psychotherapy *outside* of the organization. What if leaders were trained and had tools to use before it got that far? The recent case of the Lloyds boss leaving the bank because of stress demonstrates what happens when stress gets out of hand. Leaders taking time out because of stress are rarely seen as top leadership potential afterwards. Yet *all* leaders have times of stress and anxiety. All but two of those leaders interviewed for this book recognized periods of extreme pressure and stress and identified strongly with the concepts of Executive Gremlins.

Executive Gremlins cost companies millions of pounds a year. The best business strategies, like planes, can crash through the equivalent of pilot error. Executives themselves often cause their own best laid plans to fail.

In this book I will encourage you to think about your own strengths and needs and how acting upon your strengths and meeting these needs works for you in organizations. You will also be asked to identify real life examples of pressure and stress and you will be offered solutions which help to deconstruct these in a safe, non-threatening way.

Overview

Anxiety at the very top undermines authentic leadership at all levels of the organization and ultimately derails business strategy. So, having reflected on the views of current academic and organizational thinkers and role models, I have also included throughout the book descriptions of the dysfunctional leaders we have all encountered.

Chapter 1: Resilience under fire – Executive Gremlins are derailing your business

This chapter deals with why Executive Gremlins cause stress and anxiety in leaders and how this causes strategic change strategies to fail. Utilizing case studies from leading FTSE 500 organizations it demonstrates the importance of these issues in the context of:

- aggressive growth;
- MBO to flotation;
- joint ventures;
- recession, downsizing and internal takeovers.

Chapter 2: The secret weapon!

This chapter is the core of the book. It describes how, if a leader understands their inner worlds and insecurities (Executive Gremlins) better, they have an inherent advantage in business. It is a secret weapon because it is a capability not often mentioned in organizations, especially at the top.

Three core needs of a leader:

- the need to feel important;
- the need to be popular;
- the need to be in control of their world.

The chapter describes what happens when these and other needs are not met and how they surface as Executive Gremlins in organizations. The fears of being unimportant, unlovable, out of control, not good enough, or of being perceived as stupid, powerless or weak are the things that affect leaders and cause the poor leadership behaviours that lead to poor performance and business derailment. These topics are illustrated by case studies and autobiographical experience.

Chapter 3: Your reality is not their reality

This chapter explores the fact that we all see the world differently because we all perceive the world through our own particular set of perceptual filters. These filters arise as a result of our personal experiences from the past, which form beliefs that affect how we perceive the world. It includes a description of the thoughts and perceptions Ruby Wax and I had about each other when we first met to illustrate our own gremlins and how we were struggling to see the real people. Since we both had strong perceptual filters, we each made judgements about the other that were inaccurate. We use this as the introduction to keynote speaking engagements when we work together because it emphasizes that even seemingly successful, confident people have insecurities and needs.

The chapter also covers FEAR (False Evidence Appearing Real), conflict and assertiveness. Finally, it introduces an overview of the Executive Advantage 10-Step Solution for Resilient 21st-century Leaders© and how this can help leaders to overcome their gremlins and make better decisions in their businesses.

Chapter 4: The Executive Advantage 10-Step Solution for Resilient 21st-century Leaders©

This chapter details the process for identifying Executive Gremlins in the context of the organization and gives the reader step-by-step actions to identify a gremlin, supported by case studies from real leaders in top-tier organizations. It shows how to reframe a situation, giving you more effective strategies to use when faced with high-pressure situations. You will discover the importance of your thoughts, feelings and body language. It describes the 'aha!' or 'eureka!' moment when a gremlin is identified and how this realization leads to making new and better choices and decisions *in the moment*. It is an extremely useful chapter not only for leaders at the very top who know they have stressed executives on their boards, but also for leaders delivering at all levels in an organization, including top talent executives and executive coaches. Using this process on yourself requires high levels of emotional intelligence, and using it on others is particularly challenging. It requires leaders to have a thorough grip on their inner worlds, plus coaching skills and a robust personal toolkit before they venture into the worlds of others. Most should seek training first.

Chapter 5: Neuroleadership and the 10-Step Solution

This chapter explores current thinking on what happens in the brain when we are stressed and how different parts of the brain are activated and shut down according to our perception of threats and rewards. It explains in simple language how the brain evolved. It introduces the work of Dr David Rock and his SCARF model and how this work relates to the concept of needs and Executive Gremlins. I explore how all this relates to executive women, and how women and men are wired differently.

Chapter 6: Women on the edge

This chapter deals with the gender question and asks: 'Are women more affected by stress than men in a corporate setting?' The answer is: 'Probably not; they just show it more when they are.' The chapter reflects the recent surge in interest from CEOs and chairs following the publication of the Davies Report in 2011 (because of the implied threat of quotas). This deals with how Executive Advantage could prove particularly helpful to women seeking promotion and an improvement in confidence. It includes the findings of research undertaken specifically for this book and *Top 10 Tips for CEOs for getting more women on boards*.

Chapter 7: The rot starts at the top

This chapter deals with *how* poor leadership behaviours derail business performance. It includes discussion on:

- Authenticity and storytelling.
- Leaders who 'talk about values but don't walk the talk'.
- Factions and mafias.
- Underperforming boards, leadership teams and individual board members.
- Leaders who are off target.
- The investment in improving leadership behaviours and performance is worth it.
- Thinking longer term and bigger picture.
- Leaders must be willing to take personal risks.

This chapter also includes leader interview research conducted for this book and previous research for my doctoral thesis. Using case studies from 20 years of using The 10-Step Solution, I deconstruct how it manifests in organizations at the very top. You will recognize yourself and types of people you have worked with in organizations and start to make connections as you recall your own experiences, freeing your brain up to make better decisions next time you face similar situations and people.

Chapter 8: The Executive Advantage 21st-century Solution for organizations

In this chapter we revisit the key concerns for 21st-century leaders and the behavioural capabilities required to lead in 21st-century organizations. I explain why we need to talk about this. It provides an overview of the other capabilities – 'authentic flexibility and agility' and 'inclusive leadership' – and provides practical steps for building a positive 21st-century business culture, including mentoring programmes.

I have drawn on the experiences of CEOs and directors from FTSE 500 to SMEs. The results are remarkably consistent. Leaders at all levels in an organization from the chairman down will find something they can use in this book. My research clearly showed that all leaders relate to periods of change and stress and the pressures of working in 21st-century organizations. How well they deal with them varies. The 10-Step Solution will help you to deal with pressure and build on your strengths, aligning your personal needs with the organization's. In addition, leaders with direct responsibility for people will learn how to recognize Executive Gremlins in others and make better decisions when leading through change. We explore how these gremlins manifest in organizations going through different types of change in the next chapter.

Caveat

All the case studies in this book are real and based either on my own experience or the experiences of the leaders who contributed. I have changed the titles of the innocent and the guilty. If you are reading this book, I would ask you to imagine you had worked with me in the past – I am sure you wouldn't want me to quote you directly either! On the basis that they and I would like to work together again in the future I have respected their wishes for confidentiality – an essential prerequisite of my work. A list of most of the leaders interviewed is included.

Resilience under fire – Executive Gremlins are derailing your business

" *Anxiety at individual or organizational level always causes behaviour change. When people are under pressure you can't predict their response. They have less optimistic business plans and lose the ability to dream big. Leaders speak the right words but don't demonstrate it so people won't follow – like the Enron philosophy, 'Do whatever it takes'; leaders modelled this and look what happened.*

SUBHA BARRY, EX CHIEF DIVERSITY OFFICER, MERRILL LYNCH

Why Executive Gremlins cause strategic change programmes to fail

In this chapter I show how leadership dilemmas and decisions, good and bad, make a difference in the face of the relentless pressure in organizations. I will show what I have observed first hand – how some leaders achieve success, over and over again, whilst others with the best laid strategic plans fail to see them reach fruition due to unfulfilled needs, unresolved anxiety or Executive Gremlins driving their leadership behaviours and those of their teams.

Executive Gremlins are a major component in why strategic change programmes fail, from mergers and acquisitions, takeovers, downsizing, and aggressive growth. You will see that far from business plan failure being purely about the market, the plan, the process implementation, it is the reaction (rather than rational response) of key leaders to any given situation that makes the difference between success and failure. When challenges and disasters hit a business, it is a distinct executive advantage to understand how to control your own behaviour and that of your leaders. This creates an advantage in that once other leaders see it working at the top they emulate the behaviours and a positive culture shift occurs. Teams come together seamlessly without the usual conflict phases because everyone is behaving consistently. Confidence and resilience are improved.

In the research for this book I posed the following questions:

Have you ever experienced the derailment of a business plan, flotation or merger due to poor leadership behaviours and anxiety?

There was a lot of bullying and 'landgrabbing' when leaders were under pressure.

CEO, FTSE 500 company

The resounding answer was 'yes'; 74 per cent were able to describe experiences from their past where the poor leadership behaviours and anxiety of the CEO or another director substantially impacted the outcome. Many reported that when faced with difficult market conditions, CEOs became absent physically and refused to make decisions. They described 'executive vacuums' which paralyzed their organizations. This was particularly well described by those in the financial services industry and it resonated with my own experience. Others described conflicts between chairs and CEOs that caused politics and lack of engagement further down. Someone even described how a hedge fund manager went to an acquiring firm and sabotaged the deal.

> *Foresight is not possible in difficult circumstances – once the inner doubts start the little voice in the head saying 'Am I really any good?' leaders need something to happen externally to establish credibility internally with self so the little voice says 'Damn, I was good!'*
>
> **COO, FTSE 500 company**

The 'little voice in the head' in this case is an example of what I call an Executive Gremlin, reflecting a need to feel 'Good enough'.

Have you ever experienced feeling powerless, disregarded, unimportant, disliked or like a fraud?

> *When I received a 'shitogram' that was widely copied I felt unimportant and out of control.*
>
> **Director**

This question was asked in order to identify whether executives could relate to Executive Gremlins. Only one person could not relate to these feelings at all. Ninety per cent said they had felt 'all of them'. Many described 'imposter syndrome' (the phenomenon which occurs when someone feels they are less qualified than they should be for their position and that they may be found out as an imposter), which resonated with my feelings when first promoted to a leadership team. An example of this was that I would think of a pertinent comment in a board meeting and then second-guess how my viewpoint would land, fearing others would find my contribution (in reality me) lacking in some way, then someone else would make the same comment and everyone would say what a good point it was!

> *It was my first CEO role and I inherited a problem with a bill that failed. We were excluded from the review. I felt personally disregarded even though it hadn't been my fault. My number one priority was to regain credibility. I went out and met leaders of industry and ministers. When the bill returned we were included.*
>
> **CEO, FTSE 500 company**

In this case the underlying fear could be of being disregarded. The need was probably for status, to be recognized and feel 'Important', or it could have been for likeability, where being excluded was experienced as rejection. If we had deconstructed it using the 10-Step Solution we would have found out!

We have all heard the expression 'It's my head that's on the line' and that is truly how it feels sometimes when things are not going well. Executives feel physiological symptoms similar to those felt when we are in life-threatening situations. This is because the brain doesn't know the difference between reality and fiction. I am sure you have heard the old story: when we were cavemen, we were programmed to run away from sabre-toothed tigers when we were under threat; adrenaline and noradrenaline were released into our bloodstream and we were poised for flight. This has come to be known as 'flight or fight syndrome'. We run away or we stand and fight! Today in boardrooms across the world, executives under emotional threat experience the same physiological response. The brain cannot tell the difference between an immediate physical threat and an emotional one. Yet it is inappropriate to run away or express anger or violence in a corporate setting. We bottle it up. The resulting poor decision making and stress can lead to executive and organizational derailment. The fact that most of the world's leaders are men exacerbates this as men are even more susceptible to this phenomenon as their systems are flooded with ten times more testosterone than women. Testosterone makes them more competitive and more inclined to fight when faced with a threat situation. (I will be returning to this later in Chapter 5.) Even companies going through aggressive growth, obviously preferential to downsizing, can stimulate excessive anxiety in the drive to keep shareholder expectations under control and make target quarter on quarter whilst still trying to grow a sensible business. I will explore some of the organizations that I have seen either be successful or derail because of Executive Gremlins.

Visible leadership

Leaders must live it, own it, never doubt it.

CEO

Visible leadership is vital to resilient 21st-century organizations and achieving any sort of strategic change and commitment must be seen from the top. However, what usually happens when things get tough? The leaders disappear – either because they are paralyzed by fear and wrongly assume it is better to say nothing than to admit they don't know, or because they are too busy working externally on their business (eg when taking a flotation prospectus around the City or when looking for a buyer) to worry about what is going on internally.

> He (the CEO) withdrew and played golf. There was an authority vacuum as no one would make decisions. The FD couldn't close the books because something was wrong but he couldn't get a straight answer. When he persisted he was shouted at.
>
> **Chairman, FTSE 500 company**

In my research for this book, I also asked leaders about the importance of visible leadership – especially in times of change. 100 per cent of respondents said this was critically important, using words like 'crucial', 'hugely important', 'monumentally important'. Since they also felt that leaders withdraw under intense pressure and stress, this is worrying. This is borne out by neuroscience. Humans need certainty and look for pattern matches to make them feel comfortable. If leaders do not create certainty the brain perceives a gap and the resulting tension creates a 'button push'.

> Change management is visible leadership in the front line.
>
> **Bill Payne, vice president, CRM & industries, IBM**

There is a distinct executive advantage in being able to separate our own anxiety from what is actually going on, rather than to see a scenario through the filters of our past – filters that cause us to have negative beliefs about ourselves, which lead to knee-jerk decision making and self-interest.

This is reflected even in governments. Take Tony Blair, who kept smiling through disasters, whilst Gordon Brown skulked away. President Obama, perhaps elected through charisma, was losing his grip after a year, but was then seen to substantially raise his profile and the mood of America after the shooting of Bin Laden. Suddenly he was perceived as a visible leader to be reckoned with again.

Aggressive growth

There are many versions of organizations 'going for growth' – from MBOs going for flotation, to start-ups, joint ventures, acquisitions and mergers. For most of them the biggest pressure is not achieving growth per se but achieving it to a plan with quarter-on-quarter targets and year-on-year expectations. This is exacerbated in plc organizations as results become either a public triumph or a public humiliation for the executive board and particularly the chair and CEO.

MBO to flotation

CASE STUDY

I was involved in an MBO as HR/change director, appointed to help take the business from five people with a plan to a European company and flotation in three years. This was very exciting as it included building the organization from scratch, acquiring companies across Europe and working closely with the then MD to create innovative people solutions and strategies that supported the business plan. The MD was very visible and committed a lot of time to formulating and communicating the vision and invested in leadership training and share ownership across the company. He was not without his faults and was often in conflict personally with his other directors; however, his grasp of visibility and motivation was outstanding. He did not allow his own or other people's Executive Gremlins to get in the way of business success. He would spend hours debating the best fit and structure for different roles and departments and would also discuss his own style and how his behaviours were on some occasions not working with some of his directors. I would coach these people and try to ascertain what was going on in their world view or perception. Often their perceptions were at odds with his. Top team offsites and one-to-one coaching kept them tight as a team. The directors and leaders did well when the company floated. It is no surprise that all the mid-level leaders went on to become successful sales directors, managing directors and non-executive directors in their later careers.

The ability to look at, identify and see your own unhelpful patterns and 'gremlins' is a critical part of mastering executive advantage. It enables leaders to see when the problem is yours or someone else's or where someone needs challenging or supporting to improve performance. It sometimes seems that the board are untouchable, that they have no development needs. This is not my experience in working with them!

Joint venture

CASE STUDY

A joint venture between a telecoms giant and a European media company displayed a vision way ahead of its time: a multi-access portal linking TV, internet and mobile phones much like iPhones today – only this was the early 1990s. We launched the first interactive TV voting show and the pressure was immense, not knowing if the technology would really work until we went live. The investing parent companies were fantastic to work for but ruthless in their expectations re business performance. The JV was effectively a start-up. Start-ups are very different culturally from large corporations so there were often clashes when entrepreneurial creative types were hired with little experience of the politics of working in a big organization. Similarly, corporate types had little understanding of the media world. Egos were huge on both sides of the fence and Executive Gremlins came into play. Directors with 'Importance' needs clashed swords. We were also trying to grow market share fast, which meant acquiring companies all around Europe in a short space of time. The CEO was an ex-banker with a fantastic reputation and masses of charisma. He was excellent at building the leadership and culture of the organization and invested time and resources into it. We established a fantastic team environment with full employee engagement. I still recall the founding values. He was very self-contained and kept his emotions under control but he did not have a telecoms, IT or media background and the technology was not keeping pace with the vision. Gradually, the people who were previously willing to work all night began to lose heart and feel taken advantage of. As the timescales got shorter the pressure got greater and some people were hired at the top whose style was quite bullying and controlling, which was inconsistent with the stated values. Coaching helped a little but was not across the board and poor leadership behaviours were tolerated if business deals were done, even if they were short term in order to keep the ultimate bosses happy quarter on quarter. At this point the CEO and the board lost credibility and the workforce disengaged. They no longer believed the promises. MDs were bullying their staff because their own levels of anxiety were so high. Eventually, one of the companies bought the other half's business and absorbed it into their larger corporation.

In the example above, having started out well, this organization lost its way because of technology problems and because the executive team lost its way. Tempers would be lost, people were self-interested and politics became the order of the day. Almost all the early players left. They didn't want to play anymore. Executive Gremlins, along with technology problems, derailed the business. The technology problems could perhaps have been fixed if investors had collaborated more at the outset re expectations and renegotiated when it was apparent the vision was ahead of itself. Instead positions became entrenched. This was exacerbated by the failure of the top team to navigate through two distinct cultures, one a telecoms giant and the other a large French media company. The excitement and engagement created in the early days was lost as leaders failed to flex their personal styles. Had leaders been able to reflect on what they were doing and seen that some of their own behaviour was not helpful, then they could have changed it and calmed the chaotic feelings running riot in the company. If they could have recognized the effect their behaviour was having on others, and the Executive Gremlins they activated in their people, they could have helped people further down the chain deal with the change and the pressure.

Recession, downsizing and internal takeovers

I have experienced downsizing many times in my career – as a small business owner, as a FTSE 500 FVP, and as a change consultant brought in to facilitate change. The hardest is probably downsizing in a small business as those affected feel like family; next hardest is making part of your own team redundant in a big company whilst trying to re-engage the rest.

Perhaps the most challenging time for executives, the need to hit targets (internal or external) in a depressed market whilst cutting your own team, is harsh, and doubts about your own leadership capability and future compound this. It is in challenging times that Executive Gremlins take hold and insecurities arise.

I remember flying up to Scotland to close down an entire IT office as a young HR director, only to be met at the airport by TV cameras and crew with microphones asking me about the closure. Perhaps most alarming was that only the CEO, the global HR director and I were supposed to have known about the programme. Somehow it had leaked. My deep-seated fear of being 'unlovable' and consequent need to be liked was activated. (Whilst this may seem like an incongruous fear to be categorized as 'executive', it is quite a common one even at very senior levels.) I was, in those people's eyes, the enemy.

Handling downsizing one step removed as a consultant is a lot easier, though there are difficulties with building trust and rapport and understanding culture. However, you are still perceived as the enemy. Fortunately, I have now reached the stage in my career where I do not need to be everybody's friend!

Whatever the executive role, what appears to be key to successful handling of downsizing is building strong relationships and trust with people affected – including those affected by redundancy themselves and those left behind. This is difficult to do when you are uncertain about your own future.

An internal takeover

CASE STUDY

I was involved with a successful IT business transformation/systems integrator with a subsidiary organization that held some big government contracts. When the time came to integrate the latter I was asked to work with the board to help them to manage the process. There were a lot of egos and ruffled feathers, caused by activation of executive anxieties, but we successfully identified what was going on for each director and coached them through it and they successfully rolled out the change plans in their teams. Some time later, the acquiring company was integrated into the ultimate parent company, which stated they wanted to retain the best of them. However, it was not well handled, no investment was made in preparing the leaders for change and it largely failed. Most of the critical leaders left the business. There are many reasons for this failure, one of which was the poor handling of board members who were then unable to adequately communicate any positive messages further down. Having effectively built the company from start-up, the board were heavily invested in the company and its people. It was a sophisticated, professional, projects-based environment. When the extremely popular CEO resigned, following months of intense disagreement with the CEO of the parent company (who knew less about the subsidiary's marketplace than did the subsidiary CEO), it was the beginning of the end for the other executives. A new, bullying CEO was appointed who did not act professionally, undersold huge government projects and ultimately destroyed the heart of the business. Within a year, most of the intellectual property at the top of the organization left with the executives. Of those who are left, very few are happy and most are only staying for final salary pensions (which are now also under threat!).

Relationship and trust also break down in trades union negotiations where people's positions become entrenched – though whether this is genuinely because of executive anxiety or a form of ritualized game playing is unclear. Certainly, they appear to 'press each other's buttons' and cause considerable anxiety for management, trades union executives and workforce alike. In going through the process of de-recognizing a trades union (TGWU) some years ago, I was on a steep learning curve and probably made mistakes. Whilst we ultimately got the outcome we wanted, it was very stressful and I had to constantly manage my 'Not good enough' gremlin.

Social media, whistleblowing and breaking the brand

When anxiety gets out of hand, leading to derailment and ultimately to people leaving, the result can be a desire to get even. The upsurge in social media and social networking means that almost anyone, at any level in any organization, can become a whistleblower. Directors who were privy to confidential business plans would historically have found it very difficult to disclose information; today it is easy. Companies with strong external brands are particularly vulnerable as they have so much to lose. They invest heavily in promoting their brand and this can be lost overnight by inappropriate disclosures on social media sites such as Twitter. However, the positive side to this is that most leaders interviewed for this book said that they felt it was a good thing that people had ways of exposing poor experiences, that it essentially improved the conscience of the organization and most forward-thinking organizations encouraged people to give feedback via a process.

It is more important than ever for business leaders to ensure that they talk to people who are leaving to ascertain why and to listen to their perceived grievances. They may be unfounded or unrealistic – or they may not be. If Executive Gremlins are left unchallenged at the leadership level it may have devastating effects on the organization's market brand.

CASE STUDY

When I worked in investment banking there was an online gossip magazine that would write about the City and what the gossip was on any of the big City institutions. It became a forum for the disenchanted to air their grievances. Some people were leaving their companies and spilling the beans about company issues that would not previously have been in the public domain.

People do the same on Facebook and Twitter. Individuals can now 'break the brand' internally and externally of their organizations. Most people only do this kind of thing when they are really feeling victimized. When nobody has bothered to listen to them, or where they have been bullied and their threat response in the brain has been activated, their limbic systems or animal brains have taken over, their prefrontal cortex has shut down and they are reacting, not responding.

In order to avoid people getting even via social networking it is imperative that open, honest conversations take place, both during employment and at the point an individual exits an organization at whatever level.

Even without social media it is important to realize that our perceptions about the world are not always reality. For example, the 'glass ceiling', once a reality, is today largely perceptual. Women think it exists and worry about it and therefore it exists. I am often asked about it when presenting at women's conferences. However, when I asked the leaders about whether discrimination still exists, the response was usually 'Yes, but it's largely unconscious bias now rather than overt discrimination.' We will explore this further in Chapter 6, 'Women on the edge'.

Most of the leaders interviewed for this book agreed and felt that it was a good thing that people now had an outlet. The majority of organizations now have robust processes for dealing with grievances internally.

Bullying

I asked the question: 'Have you observed negative leadership styles?'

Ninety-eight per cent responded that they could remember working with many different types of poor leadership styles but by far the strongest was bullies and their impact on them and their organizations. One went so far as to say that he had observed it in all the organizations he had worked for. Most felt bullies lacked confidence or handled pressure badly. Women reflected that they had been bullied whilst men largely described standing up to bullies (though that doesn't mean they all do). One described a newly appointed CEO who had business experience but no understanding of the technical areas of the business, so he would focus on bullying his directors about their finances, which he did understand. Others cited 'control freaks' as the most harmful, whilst others admitted they were control freaks themselves! Most felt that these types did not engage the next layer down well and undermined succession planning. 'Know-it-alls' were described as people wanting to be 'Important' and one person described the game of who is the smartest, reflecting 'Stupid' gremlins.

I experienced being bullied by a boss. He didn't mean to be a bully. After some time out of the business due to personal problems he allowed negative feedback from a colleague with an agenda to sway his opinion of me. He had a history of being judgemental and critical of others and this time it was my turn. I am a normally balanced, healthy individual who is happy to stand up for myself but in the face of his relentless criticism, often in public, I started to lose confidence, my 'Not good enough' issues came up and I actually became less of a person and less able to shine. On one occasion he volunteered publicly to the chairman that one of my team had done all the work on a presentation we were making to the board, not me. I had in fact spent hours ploughing through the other person's work, making it more readable and a lot more succinct. I would have given him the credit anyway; the boss didn't need to do that and it embarrassed me. On another occasion he refused my request to attend a conference in the USA, saying it wouldn't be very good. I later discovered that he went himself and took another colleague of mine with him, which I would not have had a problem with if he had just said that he wanted to go. I am a normally confident individual but when I don't feel valued I start to become 'smaller' and less confident. The less like the individual he thought he had hired I became, the more angry he became, and the more he talked negatively about and to me. The more he did that, the less confident I felt. I was paralyzed and unable to confront his poor leadership behaviour. If I had, we probably would have resolved the conflict, as he is basically a good person. In fact, he is so charismatic generally that he could be a great person to work for. It was only once we got into the downward spiral of judgement and negative beliefs that it went wrong. Having worked with this individual prior to joining the company, I understood that his frustrations when he couldn't resolve a relationship in his team were based on him feeling unimportant and powerless, but it didn't help me in the moment. Despite all the work I have done on myself, I allowed my gremlins to control me. Almost all of his difficult relationships resulted in the other person leaving the company without being heard whilst others would say he was a great boss. The truth was, neither of us handled our Executive Gremlins very well. It is important in any such situation for one of the two to be the grown-up. I usually step up but on this occasion failed to. We both lost out.

CASE STUDY

I once had a coaching meeting with a FTSE 500 board director who was complaining about his bullying CEO. Then I popped to the ladies' loo, where I found a glossy notice saying bullying wouldn't be tolerated and should be reported to HR! The problem is, bullying is endemic. If the top man or woman bullies their direct reports, they may in turn bully theirs. It is a vicious cycle. In the coaching meeting in question, the director recounted how the CEO had humiliated him at a sales conference and with some work we discovered that it had activated his 'Not good enough', 'Unlovable' and 'Powerless' gremlins. Once we had identified these, he was able to see that his reaction was in fact an overreaction – he calmed down (the naming process helped his limbic system to calm down, allowing rational thought) and was able to make new decisions.

The insensitivity of the CEO and the oversensitivity of the director led to a spectacular upset. Whilst the behaviour of the CEO was 90 per cent the cause, we were able to identify that the director's own behaviour and expectations played a part. The CEO had a rampant need to feel 'Important', and demanded attention, kudos and status symbols at every turn. He was universally disliked but upset to think that people didn't like him. His own fears and behaviours were derailing his business. My client recognized that he had a need for approval, an 'Unlovable' process which was activated when he felt publicly humiliated – both because his boss made disparaging remarks and also because it happened publicly and he feared others might not like or respect him as a result.

Leaders' experiences

When the credit crunch happened I held several non-executive director positions as well as my primary role. All of them were in trouble. It was incredibly stressful. I would have continuous negative conversations in my head and couldn't sleep.

Chairman

I asked leaders about times in their careers when they had been stressed and what they do to alleviate stress. Ninety-nine per cent had examples. Most of the solutions mentioned included exercise, eating well, drinking water, meditation, breathing exercises and executive coaching. Women talked more about 'offloading' or reaching out to friends, and those who had been through tragic life experiences, like bereavement, had valued counselling. Most acknowledged that talking about it helped even if they resisted doing so initially.

I don't tend to talk to my wife about stress, I don't like to show weakness. However, sometimes she will ask a profound question and we talk and everything falls into place. When I do talk it makes me feel better. I need to take action, to do something rather than nothing. I don't want to be seen as weak or vulnerable.

Chairman

I try to stay controlled and considered, to work out what is going on, what patterns of belief might be getting in my way.

CEO

Feeling threatened through change

As a leader in a FTSE 500 company I was forced to downsize when it merged with another company. It was very difficult to keep motivating the team and stay positive when I knew that I had to cut the team by 25 per cent and also that I could lose my own job. The sword of Damacles hanging over all the leaders' heads for months increased selfishness and self-interest. Whilst some would withdraw and not talk at all (which meant people speculated on what might happen), others would gossip and share their fears, which destabilized critical players in the business. Either reaction would be provoked by any underlying fears or unhelpful beliefs held by each individual. In my case, I was happy to be paid off but, whilst I tried to remain positive, I would still question how I was being received and if I was being seen as valuable. In other cases they would start throwing their weight around, being competitive and openly dismissive of the ultimate leadership (evidencing unimportant or powerless fears). It is also extremely difficult to stay positive when information is not coming down from above, in my case the USA. It becomes difficult to hide your own emotions.

When leaders feel threatened they often withdraw and become 'paralyzed' by indecision. This is because the brain perceives a threat and the prefrontal cortex, responsible for rational thought, shuts down. The amygdala takes over, registering a threat, and the leader is unable to think clearly or make good decisions. This unsettles and destabilizes the organization further down.

Whilst there are many theories about how people respond to change, our responses are also governed by our behaviour and patterns from the past. Our underlying weaknesses as individuals surface. If we can identify these and handle them we can start to manage change at an organic level rather than as a company-wide 'sheep dip'. There are

FIGURE 1.1

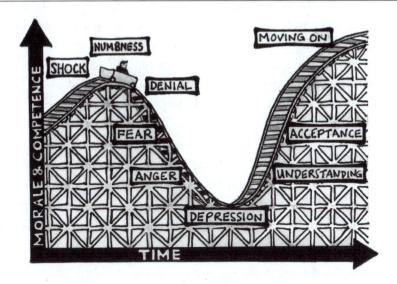

many versions of the transition curve, identified by Elisabeth Kübler-Ross, that describes the stages companies and individuals experience when going through change. The stage where this book will be helpful is when you have reached the emotional stage and are attempting to step into exploring options for the future. (The transition curve, sometimes called the grief cycle, sees people going through several stages through organizational change from denial, to emotion, to exploration and ultimately to acceptance.) It is easier to be precise about what is driving unhelpful behaviours at this stage than when people are in denial as emotions and thoughts need to be identified in order to label the Executive Gremlin at work and work out ways of overcoming it. I have used the metaphor of a roller coaster to illustrate the way our emotions go up and down through the change curve. It is very important to stay on track!

Why is it important to talk about change?

Leadership experts have been talking about change for decades. However, the pressure in the 21st century is building. Pace, agility, globalization and 24/7 cultures mean change is constant. It is relentless and leaders need a mechanism for managing it that really works. The Executive Advantage 10-Step Solution is such a mechanism. If they can identify and handle their own gremlins, they can substantially speed up their people's journey through the change curve and help to avoid them spiralling down into negative emotion and depression. People do not like change imposed upon them; they need to feel in control as much as possible. Our brains look for pattern matches, so when confronted with something different from what we know, a threat response is triggered and we resist. Leaders with high status needs will find it particularly challenging when confronted with faits accomplis. Authentic flexibility and resilience are particularly important in helping them deal with the realities of 21st-century organizational life.

In recent years the worlds of psychology (the study of the mind – which thinks, feels and acts – and human behaviour) and neuroscience (the study of the anatomy and physiology of the brain) have started to merge. Scans have revealed neural connections. We now know that leadership behaviour in the workplace doesn't always work in the way we think it does. This is why change programmes fail and why it is possible to substantially improve the success of a change project by working with the natural predisposition of employees' brains. David Rock and Jeffrey Schwartz came up with the following conclusions in their paper 'The Neuroscience of Leadership':

- *Change is pain.* Organizational change is unexpectedly difficult because it provokes sensations of physiological discomfort. (The brain cannot tell the difference between physical pain and social pain.)
- *Behaviourism doesn't work.* Change efforts based on incentive and threat (the carrot and stick) rarely succeed in the long run.
- *Humanism is overrated.* In practice, the conventional empathic approach of connection and persuasion doesn't sufficiently engage people.

- *Focus is power.* (What we focus on expands.) The act of paying attention creates chemical and physical changes in the brain.

- *Expectation shapes reality.* People's preconceptions have a significant impact on what they perceive (see Chapter 3, 'Your reality is not their reality').

- *Attention density shapes identity.* Repeated, purposeful and focused attention can lead to long-lasting personal evolution.

All over the world, companies spend millions trying to sweep up the mess caused by failure of their organizations to flex, adapt and change. At the core of these failures lie poor leadership behaviours and poor decision making. The top team of any organization are role models who set the culture and the tone for their businesses. This may be a good thing or a bad thing! If leaders can identify what the core causes of their own behaviours are, and the underlying Executive Gremlins driving them, and develop strategies for their resolution, they will be able to create considerable executive advantage for their businesses. In Chapter 2 we will explore how leadership behaviours, good and bad, have affected organizations and I will introduce 'The secret weapon'.

The secret weapon!

Understanding how your Executive Gremlins affect your success, and that of your bosses and colleagues, may be one of the most useful tools in the executive toolkit. It goes to the heart of why leaders fail. The reason it is called the secret weapon is that not all leaders have this capability. It is a subject rarely talked about in organizations, either because people fear it shows weakness or because organizations fear that if they acknowledge that the pressure of leadership roles cause individuals to experience stress, and if this leads to an individual taking legal action for compensation, it will open the floodgates to legal action by dozens of other aggrieved executives. Skilled 21st-century leaders use this weapon to create an advantage for their own careers and for the success of their companies. In order to help people understand their inner fears and gremlins, I label them. The effect of identifying and labelling actually has the effect of reducing the fear state and emotion in the brain as the limbic system, responsible for emotion, dampens down, making us more receptive to change.

Human needs and Executive Gremlins

Executive Gremlins come about as a result of human needs not being met. We are born with needs and we acquire more as we grow, according to the experiences we have and the environment we live in. The Human Givens Institute developed a set of organizing ideas, developed by Joe Griffin and Ivan Tyrrell, that provide a holistic and scientific framework for understanding the way individuals and society work.

They believe that we come into the world with a set of needs (hence the name) and that, if these needs are met appropriately, it will be impossible to be mentally ill, suffer with depression or have addictions. Their work builds upon the work of Sigmund Freud, Alfred Adler and Abraham Maslow, whose work has been widely referenced in organizations. Maslow believed that until humans' basic needs are met, people will not be able to engage with questions of meaning and spirituality – what he calls self-actualization. The work of William Glasser proposed that the fulfilment of people's needs for control, power, achievement and intimacy depends on their ability to behave responsibly and conscientiously. He argued that if these needs are not met, mental illness occurs. All these thinkers, and many more, have explored the world of human needs.

Emotional needs

- *Security* – safe territory and an environment which allows us to develop fully;
- *Attention* – to give and receive it;
- *Sense of autonomy and control* – the freedom to make our own choices;
- *Emotional intimacy* – knowing that others accept us for who we are;
- *Feeling part of a wider community*;
- *Privacy* – an opportunity to reflect and consolidate experience;
- *Sense of status within social groups*;
- *Sense of competence and achievement*;
- *Meaning and purpose*.

The resources we have to help us meet our needs include:

- *The ability to develop complex long-term memory* – which allows us to add experience;
- *The ability to build rapport, empathize and connect with others*;

- *Imagination*, which enables us to focus our attention away from emotions and problem solve;

- *Emotions and instincts*;

- *A conscious rational brain that can check our emotions, analyze and plan*;

- *The ability to 'know'* – to understand the world unconsciously through pattern matching;

- *An observing self* – the ability to stand back and be objective.

My research into leadership has led me to the conclusion that it is the way deep-seated human needs and fears are expressed in the context of highly stressful organizational settings that is unique, not that they are fundamentally different from fears as treated by psychotherapists in other settings. I also recognize in saying this that what I describe as Executive Gremlins are typically experienced by so-called 'normal' people, rather than by people who have been diagnosed as having a mental illness that might be treated by psychotherapists in other settings. Dynamic, seemingly successful leaders often experience crises of confidence. Underneath our acts are basic human fears. We will often deny their existence; however, they show up in executives' lives in a number of ways: the need for respect and oversensitivity to being disregarded (likely Executive Gremlin: Unimportant), to needing a long list of qualifications and having to say something on every subject (likely Executive Gremlin: Stupid), to fear of presenting (likely Executive Gremlin: Unlovable and/or Unimportant) to playing politics and bullying staff whilst sucking up to the boss (likely Executive Gremlin: Powerless). These fears may lead to self-questioning about 'Who am I?' and 'How can I make a difference?' particularly as we reach retirement or when facing redundancy.

These fears manifest as a result of our own personal journeys and life experiences from the past, which form our belief systems and create filters that influence how we perceive our present and future situations and possibilities. Once CEOs and executives learn to manage their own anxieties, they can positively affect the performance of their boards and their companies. This will in turn affect the leadership of the organization and becomes a significant executive advantage.

Belief systems – where do they come from?

As babies and small children we all experience positive and negative influences and situations and these combine to form particular stress triggers or fears, the limiting self-beliefs we have about ourselves, based on our experiences from the past.

FIGURE 2.1

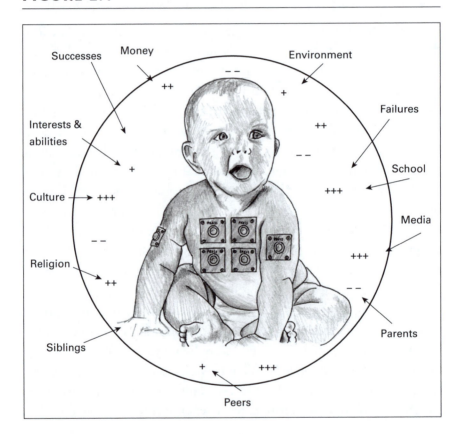

As adults, our limiting and enabling beliefs form filters through which we perceive the world. We look for evidence to prove our beliefs and ignore anything that does not fit with our preconceived perceptions (hence prejudice thrives). New evidence then strengthens the original filter until we are totally convinced of the 'truth' before us. An extreme example of this would be an anorexic person looking into a mirror and seeing a fat one. Another would be the belief that all people of a certain race are criminals. In the corporate setting, a sales director who believes that the next quarter will be better, when all the evidence points to failure, is seeing their situation through different filters from their board's! When I present at leadership conferences and ask how many executives would like to be on the board of a plc, about two-thirds of the hands go up. When I qualify it by asking how many believe they will be, many of the hands go down. This is the effect of limiting self-beliefs creating filters. They just don't recognize that they are 'Good enough' (and whilst some may not be, many who are self-doubt). This type of distorted belief, driven by Executive Gremlins, affects executives working in organizations. By helping them to identify what they are, and giving them helpful strategies for coping, they are freed up to make new choices. In addition, the stressful nature of today's corporate environment leads to people bottling up their emotions.

Have you ever misread a situation due to preconceived beliefs?

Our CEO had an executive coach who also worked with his board. The board members didn't like this coach and were not cooperating. As a result, I had the preconceived notion that this coach was more disruptive than helpful but it turned out I was wrong – in the end he did a really great job.

Group HR director

These questions went to the heart of my proposition – that our pre-existing belief systems form filters through which we perceive the world. We look for evidence to validate our existing beliefs, and the filters ensure that is all we see. These form patterns which our brains recognize, sometimes erroneously because our brains are recognition machines: they will take the best pattern match rather than look for contrary evidence. Leaders must be willing to look for contrary evidence. For instance, in the area of Inclusion, when we look for 'the best' candidates we often look at the options through our own filters, which by their very nature must include bias because they create our unique perceptions. Most people agreed that there is very little conscious bias any more. However, the unconscious bias that exists is due to these unhelpful filters. Training in inclusive leadership, rather than just 'tick-box' online diversity programmes that protect companies from litigation, is necessary.

The emotional bucket

FIGURE 2.2

We can use the metaphor of the emotional bucket to describe this. If you imagine you have an emotional bucket inside you, each time you receive a negative emotional blow such as being overlooked for promotion, your partner leaving you, or being made redundant, this reinforces your fears and your negative beliefs and puts more 'stuff' into your bucket. Eventually, you are walking around with a full bucket. It then only takes a tiny drip more to cause a huge, out of proportion, reaction. Many executives today are walking around with full emotional buckets. I had one client who cried every time she walked into the room for her first three coaching sessions. She never cried at work and claimed the only other person to have seen her upset was her husband. She had a 'full bucket' and just knowing she was going to 'share', together with feeling safe in our relationship, caused the outpouring before she could deal with talking about her emotions. It did not last for long; if it had, I would have suggested taking a counselling route with her rather than continuing with coaching, as there would clearly have been deeper issues that would not have been appropriate to deal with in an organizational setting.

I am not proposing that senior executives encourage people to emote to this degree, nor are most qualified to do so. But it is an illustration of how much stress some executives are under and where they need to be aware enough to notice when a colleague may need outside interventions in order to cope.

Executive Gremlins also contribute to success. The need to feel important may drive an executive to obtain promotion. The fear of looking stupid may encourage us to study and gain qualifications. The need to feel loved may create genuinely nice people as we want to be liked! Executive Gremlins help people to achieve and succeed in business as they provide the impetus to work hard to meet our needs. However, executives may have divided loyalty about their resolution. They may subconsciously fear that if they resolve the fears that drive them, they could end up being less powerful. It is a leap of faith to tackle them and there is an existential risk involved. Executives may only be ready to tackle them when the pain of not changing becomes unbearable.

Some executives suffer with a fear of success. Rather than feeling a failure, which is perhaps more in keeping with someone who feels inside that they are not good enough or powerless, they may find that, when opportunities arise, they subconsciously sabotage situations. Fear of success may be just as paralyzing as fear of failure. Many leaders fear success because it tests their limits and makes them vulnerable. They may fear weaknesses will be exposed. Success is scary because it still involves change, which may lead to the brain experiencing a threat response. Fear of success raises the

Executive Gremlin of 'Not good enough' and 'Stupid' – the little voice in the head is saying 'Can I live up to this success?'

CASE STUDY

A colleague of mine who is currently poised to capitalize on her success told me that when she signed papers for sponsorship of her organizations with a major bank, she felt flat and like she had a mountain to climb. She said she was prepared for facing the failure of it falling through but not the fear of being successful.

Key signs of fear of success

- *Procrastinating* and putting off challenging decisions in favour of insignificant tasks;
- *Sabotaging yourself* the night before a big board meeting or presentation (eg by drinking or staying up late);
- *Lack of self-discipline* to follow through on goals and actions;
- *Pessimism and negativity* – not trying and focusing on what's wrong rather than what's right.

In order to help people to identify their patterns and beliefs, I labelled their core fears or Executive Gremlins as follows:

Executive Gremlin: Unimportant

This is perhaps the need that surfaces most in organizations. It shows up in the presenting issues of being undermined in some way including:

- *being ignored* (eg not being invited to a meeting or being left off an e-mail distribution list), of being excluded (eg 'You don't need to come to this meeting' or 'This is not a project we need you involved in');

- *not being respected* (eg an interim changing a board report without reference to the originating author), being criticized in any way for whatever reason in public, even when justified (eg being called to account for not delivering);

- *being passed over in deference to another* (eg where an issue is discussed with the executive's boss before it is raised directly with them) and finally, when being kept waiting.

CASE STUDY

A first vice president of a global pharmaceutical company presents as a well-balanced executive who is very in control of her environment. We started our coaching intervention by working on leadership goals and goals relating to her career. However, as our coach–client relationship developed, so did her willingness to expose fears and vulnerability. On one occasion she shared that one of her employees was going round her to her ultimate superior in the USA. We worked on the presenting issue and identified that by doing that her direct report had triggered my client's internal need to feel important. On another occasion, she was enraged whilst on maternity leave because the person covering for her had changed a board report that she had spent the last six years developing without asking for her permission. We explored the fact that she had not specified that he could not make changes in her (eight and a half months') absence from work without checking with her and that it was entirely possible that he was trying to make improvements, not to undermine her. Her response was to not make an issue of it and to let it go. We explored the nature of passive–aggressive behaviour and she eventually decided that if it was important enough to make her that angry it was likely that she would need to confront both her own feelings and the issue in a non-aggressive way, rather than by avoiding it. By undertaking my process we were able to identify that she had an Unimportant gremlin and more useful ways to address it.

Individuals with this particular fear often appear to be successful and motivated. They are constantly seeking positive reinforcement of their position in life. They are often, though not always, directors with the trappings of importance, like fast cars, big offices and designer clothes. In their personal lives they frequently have relationship problems, often being in second relationships or no relationship at all, having a constant need for affirmation from new people. Finally, there are the people who are married or living with very dominant husbands or wives, who feel neglected and unimportant at home and who then feel the need to feel more important at work. The 'little voice in the head' driven by this fear speaks of low self-esteem and feelings of inadequacy. In my experience, even the most confident-seeming individuals have a 'little voice in the head' that puts them down and causes self-doubt. In order to prove to themselves that they *are* important, people with the fear of being Unimportant will at times resort to bullying and aggression, which leads them to being feared in the organization. They will be perplexed to discover that they are unpopular and feared by others and still fail to get the acknowledgement they seek. This then provides further evidence for the internal fear that they are Unimportant and the fear becomes stronger. Unfortunately, this then strengthens the Unimportant lens through which they perceive the world and they are then even more likely to look for slights and evidence that others do not view them as important.

Other Executive Gremlins that are similar to and often link to the core fear of being 'Unimportant' include: 'Not good enough', 'Insignificant' and 'Powerless' or 'Weak'. Many executives in the UK suffer with the 'Not good enough' fear which leads to us experiencing impostor syndrome mentioned previously, questioning whether we are in fact good enough. We are constantly trying to prove to ourselves and to others that we *are* good enough, hence our willingness to put up with poor work–life balance and stress levels. I have heard CEOs and chairmen say that they have a fear that one day they will be found out as being an impostor, a reflection of a 'Not good enough' fear.

Executive Gremlin: Unlovable

The need to feel loved is universal. Like all Executive Gremlins, our personal experiences of loss in childhood and the patterns of behaviour of parents, siblings, peers and school all have an impact on the emergence of our limiting self-beliefs and unhelpful perceptual lenses and mental maps. In adult life this gremlin manifests as:

- *an inability to trust*, which often causes second-guessing and politicking in organizations;
- *feelings of being unsafe*, which cause paranoia;
- *constantly questioning the motivations of others*;
- *feeling undermined by others in a meeting*;
- *feeling disregarded at not being invited to a meeting* (similar to the unimportant fear, but driven by a different gremlin);
- *fearing someone else will take the credit for their work* (being overlooked);
- *being in conflict with others* (when actually they are hurt);
- *indecisiveness about whether they should stay in their jobs* when they are being 'courted' by headhunters. (People with this gremlin are particularly susceptible to being flattered and to overtures of friendship.)

The positive side to people with an 'Unlovable' gremlin is that they tend to be very popular with others as they try so hard to be liked. They invest huge amounts of energy into making other people happy. Unfortunately, they are often disappointed by colleagues and friends, who may not try so hard. Their issues with trust lead them to making judgements about others' motivations that then actually create problems in relationships. One of the most valuable interventions of the leader is in helping individuals to recognize when they are overreacting to a relationship issue, where their internal process is so strong that they read things into a situation that aren't there. Research shows us that people leave bosses, not organizations. This is also a fear which causes people upset in their personal lives and the leader may need to suggest external help when presented with executives with marriage problems, having affairs, in conflict with ex-spouses, as these things substantially impact on executive performance. This gremlin resonates with the relational needs expressed in David Rock's SCARF model, which is explored further in Chapter 5.

I grew up in a male-dominated family who, like most families in those days, were not particularly emotionally or physically demonstrative. My father worked a lot, providing for us, and I believed my mother was closer to my older brother. I have clear memories of feeling alone and unloved. I became a rebel, my attempt to get my parents' attention. I believed my parents hated me. My father became controlling, negative and involved for the first time in my life and I resented this. My brother was my most positive role model but was unfortunately killed in a car crash. This added further evidence to my unlovable process (that if I allow myself to love someone they will leave me). When I reached 17 years old, in total conflict with everyone except my brother, my mother said to me 'We are only like this because we love you' and I started to believe they really did love me. I don't remember being told that before then, though I am sure they must have. I met my future husband aged 18 and we had a long-distance but UK-based relationship until I started work as a trainee solicitor in the City and he bought a charter yacht. I happily followed him to sea and worked on the yacht for two years, giving up my 'boring' job. Basically, I was not secure enough to let him live on the other side of the world for half the year as I thought I would lose him. This was my first demonstration of my Executive Gremlin of being unlovable at work in my career. I gave up my career to follow his. Later, I worked my way up in HR. Despite being viewed as 'a strong career woman', my career choices were characterized by needing strong relationships that gave me approval. Where these were missing, I looked for another job. Being offered new jobs made me feel 'special' and of value and I made career choices based on this. I was a popular and effective HR director as I was able to understand the other person's perspective and what would motivate whole teams and organizations, especially through change and business transformation. My internal sensitivity, which was so painful in my inner world, became helpful in the cut-and-thrust world of business.

Other fears that can link with an 'Unlovable' gremlin include the fear of being Weak, Fat, Not good enough, Ugly, or Powerless. The exact nature of these fears will be unique to each person depending on their internal process and experiences. People with extreme unlovable fears may feel that life is not worth living, that they are nobody when a relationship breaks down or they are made redundant. Again, this threatens their existential significance. *If work, or my relationship, is taken away, what or who is left? How do I define myself?*

CASE STUDY

A strategy director for a large telecoms company was successful at work but got passed over for promotion on more than one occasion. He was frustrated by this as he perceived he did a good job. We identified that he would hold himself back in meetings for fear of saying the wrong thing and feared he would look stupid. Underpinning this fear of looking stupid was the bigger fear of being unlovable. When we identified this we were able to work on strategies to overcome this – like meeting other board members before meetings to assess their reaction in advance so that he was not hit with a 'button press' in the meeting itself. He was also able to lobby for support and to build stronger relationships with his colleagues. His unlovable fear was also paralyzing him at home. His wife was exchanging intimate text messages with a mutual friend and although he didn't want to believe she was having an affair, he suspected it. We explored this to identify what was real and what was just his fear. He had been unable to deal with this for months and it was causing him difficulties at work. By the process of explicating and handling his executive fear, he was able to finally confront (with himself as well as with his wife) that she was actually having an affair. We were then able to work through the whole process of divorce, children, houses, money, and he is now happily in a relationship with a new partner, living in his own home with child access. This is common to most executive fears. It is in the 'holding back' from feeling the emotion around them that is the most painful. Once we accept the fact that we need to confront it, and feel the feelings, the process of freeing up from our fears can happen.

Executive Gremlin: Control

This is not a big fear area for me. I am comfortable taking risks and with thinking outside the box. I delegate and expect people to handle things and usually enjoy good working relationships as a result. At home I am similarly relaxed. My issues with control are usually when someone else attempts to control me. I have never enjoyed working with superiors or with clients who micro manage, preferring the flexibility to get results in a variety of ways. Working with subordinates with a high need for structure and control is also a problem as I am not detailed enough to support them.

This fear is very prevalent in today's business world. The pace of change, the speed of communication (mobile phones, smartphones, the internet) and the sheer complexity and nature of today's business environments make it impossible to keep control of everything and yet we still try. This particular fear manifests in presenting issues like:

- 'I have no work–life balance.'
- 'My subordinates are all going home early whilst I am working weekends.'
- 'Colleagues complain I am a bottleneck.'
- 'I have to make unreasonable demands upon my people but someone has to get the work done.'
- 'I have been passed over for promotion because they say I need to be more strategic.'
- 'How do I really add value as a director when there is so much firefighting to do?'
- 'Don't challenge me or the status quo.'

At a deeper personal level it shows up in fearing illness and death, of not having enough money to retire, of having to do things 'my way'. Some readers may remember the article 'Who's got the monkey?'

by William Oncken, Jr and Donald L Wass. This is about the idea that leaders often take on all the problems of their people and then become a bottleneck. For those that were not around when this work was first published, it involves the idea that in any organization we all have different types of work to do – some self-imposed, some imposed by bosses, subordinates and peers. Monkeys are problems or management tasks. They live on our backs. As leaders we have to be careful not to acquire other people's monkeys! Imagine you are walking down a corridor and someone greets you and tells you about their problem. You realize you have enough knowledge to get involved but not enough to make an instant decision. As you are busy but you don't want to be rude, you say 'Let me think about that and get back to you.' They go away happy because the next action is now yours – you have taken on their monkey! If you keep taking on others' monkeys you will become overloaded and a bottleneck. Other people start checking if you have done things and you are under more pressure. Today, monkeys have grown into the size of gorillas! The sheer size and complexity of global companies make it impossible for leaders to control everything. The challenge is to leave people with their monkeys but help them with them. You will need to explain the following:

> " *At no time while I am helping you with this or any other problem will your problem become mine. The minute your problem becomes mine you will no longer have a problem and I can't help someone who hasn't got a problem!*

You will need to schedule time to follow up but they will return only at appointed times and under control. You will have control of your calendar again without overcontrolling the situation.

People with a high need for control encourage dependency in others and become 'martyrs', constantly complaining about how they are the only people who can do something. At home they can be fiercely possessive and demanding and often have obsessively tidy homes and rituals that must be observed. They are usually structured and organized, however, and do get things done at work and at home. One of the most vivid descriptions of a person with a strong fear of losing control was the film about the life of Joan Crawford's stepdaughter Christina (1981), based on a book written by her step-daughter, detailing the compulsive, controlling and abusive be-haviour she and her brother endured at the hands of their adoptive mother.

This is not uncommon; if the person needing to be in control is the boss, they will fire people who are good but who challenge them. If they are the subordinate, they tend to get fired or moved to other roles. Controlling individuals often surround themselves with 'yes men' who just reinforce their fears that they have to do everything. In their personal lives, controlling individuals may have submissive partners and co-dependent relationships. They may also have rebel-lious children seeking to spread their wings. Alternatively, they have unadventurous offspring who find it very difficult to make decisions as they have never been allowed to do so in the past. It is interesting to note that quite a few leaders interviewed said they were control freaks, so it has obviously worked in their favour too!

CASE STUDY

Many years ago I was involved in a management buyout with a team of five. We successfully built it from a £3 million company to £14 million in eight countries with over 400 staff. At the end of three years we floated the company. I was HR director and worked easily and happily with the then MD – a control freak, to use one of the more polite terms of the rest of the board. He was very effective when the company was small as he knew what to do and how to grow. He inspired people and encouraged and motivated them. He invested in identifying his vision and rolling out a culture programme. I became a right-hand man and became his unofficial sounding board. The nature of my personality and my role meant that I was happy to let him have his say and to be flexible but as he had less personal knowledge of my areas than, say, sales and marketing (his background), I was allowed more freedom to act. He would interfere and dominate and argue with everything his other key directors attempted to do. Much of my time was spent handling conflict between directors and him. It was here that I learned firsthand about conflict resolution. When we explicated his fear, we identified that he was afraid of losing everything. He came from a very poor background and had worked his way up. His wife left him with a two-year-old son and he worked and brought him up alone. He did not trust easily and believed that the company would fall apart without him. Whilst this was undoubtedly true in the early entrepreneurial years, it became less so as the company grew and an infrastructure was established. He would not have made a good MD once the company became a plc. Fortunately, for him and the business, when his company floated he became a multimillionaire and retired to Australia.

Control freaks can often do a good job for a period of time as they get things done, are organized and thorough. However, if two people with control issues try to come together in a work environment it can be very unproductive as more time is spent deciding whose way is the best way than in getting the job done. This happened with this particular individual and his sales director. Although the sales director was successful, he would not compromise his authority for the sake of his relationship with the MD. Despite coaching him, it became obvious that they would not be able to work together and the SD resigned.

Working with people with this fear entails encouraging and questioning them around how they can loosen the reins and allow others more authority and responsibility. It is important that they develop coping strategies and that they visualize ahead – looking at beneficial outcomes rather than the detailed steps required to maintain control. Other fears often associated with this fear are Untrustworthy, Weak, Unsafe (a lot of people who have had abusive or absent parents have this one) and Not good enough.

Learning to handle your gremlins

Handling Executive Gremlins is not an easy process. I have a robust 'personal toolkit'. I have trained in numerous methodologies and have a wide background of experience. I use all of this in my work with Executive Gremlins, helping leaders to explore their inner worlds and explicating their fears by incisive questioning and listening. When they have identified and labelled the gremlin, we work out ways of handling and coping with them. It may be necessary to revisit the issue over and over again in different ways until they reach an insight, or they may make a connection straight away, depending on how strong the trigger is and how open or defended the person is. I am not advocating that leaders attempt to work with their people on these straight from reading this book. You need to work on your own first! However, an understanding of the principles, being able to handle yourself, to be present and responsive to other people's needs and insecurities is a powerful executive advantage, especially when facing crises of confidence around stepping up, going for promotion and feeling more confident. We have looked at some core Executive Gremlins in this chapter. The Executive Advantage 10-Step Solution for Resilient 21st-century Leaders© helps leaders to identify what is going on in stressful situations, with themselves and with those around them. This helps them to make new, better choices and decisions which in turn result in better leader and organizational performance. It is explained in detail in Chapter 4.

Your reality is not their reality

CASE STUDY

In one client organization I observed a CEO convinced that his business was doing well even though he repeatedly faced a hostile group board who did not think so and regularly gave him this feedback. He also believed his operational board were loyal team members when they were anything but, going behind him to the shareholders and engineering his removal from the business. He simply couldn't see the reality of the situation because he felt under threat and needed to convince himself that 'everything would be OK'.

We all have our own 'view of the world'. This is based on our personal journey and life experiences, which form our belief systems and create filters that influence how we perceive our present and future situations and possibilities. This can lead to us having a distorted view of a situation and is one of the reasons why people in organizations lack confidence and get into conflict. They will enter into a situation and view it completely differently from another person because their perception of events is different due to their own personal beliefs. Fear has been defined as in Figure 3.1.

Fear causes us to perceive situations incorrectly, to see 'evidence' before us that validates fear, rather than reality. Executives can substantially improve their promotion prospects just by looking for evidence that confirms their capabilities rather than their flaws.

FIGURE 3.1

False

Evidence

Appearing

Real

As we have seen, as babies and small children we all experience positive and negative influences and situations. These combine to form either positive enabling perceptions about ourselves or to form Executive Gremlins – negative, limiting self-beliefs. These create patterns that the brain will recognize every time a fear is triggered. In such instances the brain will perceive a threat and an automatic response will take place. Even if the new situation is not actually threatening, the brain will still perceive it as such.

FIGURE 3.2

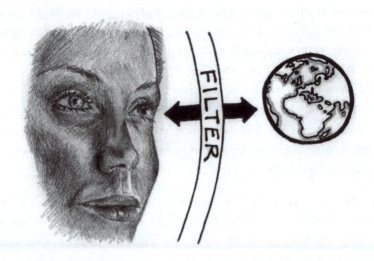

Your reality and conflict

When we get into conflict we tend to look at the situation only from our own perspective, through our own filters or lenses. We all tend to look for what is wrong with the other person in order to feel right about our own behaviour. There is a saying I learned from a wise mentor: 'Be willing to be wrong and happy,' ie believe that sometimes it is OK for someone else to be right. One of the key ways of handling conflict is to 'look at your own part', to see where your own behaviour is not helping a situation. Even if the other party is 90 per cent at fault in a conflict situation, there is still the remaining 10 per cent that is still yours. Just by engaging with it you are contributing to it. Very few people can have an argument if the other person is not reacting!

CASE STUDY

I worked with another CEO that was constantly in conflict with his operating board. One after another board member was proved, in his mind, a 'problem person'. He would spend hours with me (I was his HR director) debating his strategies to deal with them and I spent hours trying to hold up the mirror, to help him see that his behaviour was not helping, without alienating him. Too much feedback and I would become the enemy, not enough and he would have continued to clash swords with his team. We tackled some of these issues on top team offsite workshops and some we worked on privately. Perhaps the most valuable discovery he made during his tenure was the Executive Gremlin (Unimportant) that caused him to try to control and dominate others. Once we had identified this we were able to work on more helpful strategies for his leadership day to day.

Exploders, stuffers and covert stabbers

When we are in conflict with others, we all react in one of the following three ways, which define us as:

- *Exploders*. Exploders show their anger and don't think in the moment of consequences. This happens when an Executive Gremlin has been triggered and an 'amygdala hijack' has occurred. (This happens when the brain perceives a threat and the prefrontal cortex shuts down, and the amygdala, part of the limbic system, the animal part of our brains, takes over. Consequently, we are no longer able to make rational decisions and we attack.) Bullies are often exploders.

- *Stuffers*. Stuffers internalize their reactions, only letting their anger show when they are pushed beyond reason. However, they can still be experiencing the same brain response; it is just less obvious to other people, which is why people are so surprised when a 'stuffer' attacks. This is what happens when abused spouses finally react to their abusive partners.

- *Covert stabbers*. These people will attack you but it is hidden behind attacking sarcastic words. People in competition often do this. They put down the other person in public. This often occurs as a form of emotional leakage. As they are unable to directly confront a situation, they display their hostility by their remarks and sarcasm.

The assertiveness pendulum

Figure 3.3 illustrates the swing that takes place between passive and aggressive behaviour. Most people are naturally predisposed towards one side of the pendulum. If more comfortable on the passive side, they will take a lot of abuse before finally exploding, often inappropriately, at another person. After this they will then swing back to being passive as they feel guilty. Those who are more naturally found on the aggressive side of the pendulum will push and bully until someone or something raises their inappropriate behaviour to consciousness and then feel guilty and swing over to the passive side, usually making excuses for their behaviour. Whichever the tendency, in most situations neither is appropriate and what is most effective is the assertive position in the middle. This can be particularly hard

FIGURE 3.3

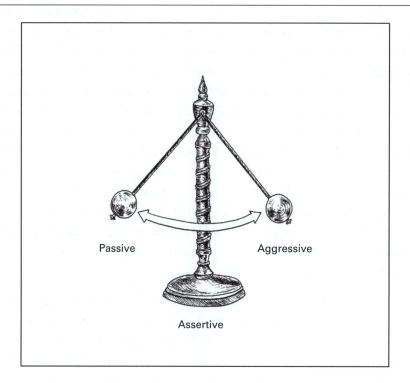

Passive   Aggressive

Assertive

if the situation is especially stressful. Addressing poor behaviour without attacking is perhaps the most difficult thing to do.

If you ignore top team conflict it will not go away

I am often astounded at how many powerful, able chairmen and CEOs talk to me about top team conflicts but seem to feel that these are an insurmountable problem. These normally fantastic role models are helpless in the face of conflict when they usually take extremely complex business issues easily in their stride. They will spend ages pondering over whether to remove an underperforming sales director or a poor MD when they would make a market or supplier decision in a fraction of that time. They will often seek to gain agreement and counsel from others to help them feel OK about their decision. And yet, usually they already *know* what needs to be done.

They are looking for validation. They don't want to feel bad about their decision. Similarly, they don't want to 'front up' poor behaviour in a direct manner as they don't want to rock the boat or for the non-execs to hear of it. So it is swept under the carpet. Yet similar conflicts arise over and over, just prompted by different organizational symptoms. They often manifest when two or more directors have importance issues (as in the CEO example above). They will constantly be trying to prove to themselves and to each other that they are the more important alpha person. (I use the term advisedly as there are plenty of women with importance issues as well as more stereotypical men.) This can lead to competition, a contest which has its foundations in self-doubt and insecurity. A confident person does not need to compete with or undermine others. However, even placid and well-balanced individuals can be pushed past their limits by a persistent offender!

Executive Gremlins are activated when we *overreact* to a situation. Where an external stimulus occurs and the average person would respond at 50 per cent, a person with any sensitivity in this area will respond at 70–80 per cent and someone who is very defended and un-self-aware may respond at 100 per cent, though this is rare in business. In which case, we are more sensitive in this area than others so our reactions are out of proportion to the event. If two people are in conflict and busy 'pushing each other's buttons' they will both be talking at the other, with neither listening.

LEAP!

I developed this mnemonic to help any leader in business handle a conflict situation. It is very simple but very helpful, as both parties feel heard. It is suitable to apply when you are one of the conflicted people but quite difficult if emotions are running high so it may be sensible to ask someone else to facilitate the discussion. Despite its simplicity, I have found this to help at the most senior levels of organizations.

FIGURE 3.4

L	Listen to each person's point of view (one at a time, no interrupting)
E	Evaluate the situation and clarify your understanding
A	Ask each to propose solutions and reach agreement
P	Plan to implement new agreements and behaviours

CASE STUDY

I used this in an organization where two lawyers were in conflict. First I explained the process and took them through each step, reminding them that each of them would have a turn and that they must listen and not interrupt when the other was speaking. Then we took each step in turn. Each 'ran out' their version of events and the other listened. Then they were able to comment on each other's point of view and evaluate what they had heard. This was the most contentious part. I reminded them of the rules and kept them on track. After some discussion we agreed the solution and put actions in place. They were never best friends but part of the solution was to split their workload differently so they did not have to work together day to day. They were able to have a resilient conversation that led to better working practices for them and their teams.

The bottom line is that this will only work once people are calm enough to discuss the issues. Neuroscientists have shown that we only perceive 'friend or foe' and that once we perceive a threat our animal brain will take over from our rational brain. The prefrontal cortex, responsible for rational thought, will shut down, making it difficult to think straight, whilst the amygdala, responsible for the threat response, is sending danger signals. The limbic system, responsible for emotion, takes over. So this process provides a helpful framework for reaching a solution once both parties are calm and wish to do so. It may be necessary to have a 'time out' for this to occur. Where beliefs about the other are so entrenched that they do not want this, it is time to work with them individually to discover which deep-seated issues are involved. Again, expert advice may well be needed in this case.

CASE STUDY

Two directors of an organization were determined to oust a senior board director. The board director in question was underperforming and the group chairman was trying to make the right decision. His dilemma was whether the individual could be turned around in time to do what was needed in the business. The two directors influencing this were entrenched in their views with strong negative beliefs about her. They involved people reporting to her, which led to a loss of respect for her, which threatened her position as a leader. There were factions in the business and ultimately they won and the board director was exited. The two directors were not self-aware and lost some respect from the group board in the process. It was probably the right long-term decision for the business, handled poorly. The Executive Gremlins of 'Unimportant', 'Unlovable' and 'Not good enough' were in play. There is still conflict within this business and it inhibits wider staff engagement and growth.

When Ruby met Jacqui

Ruby Wax and I speak at conferences on the subject of my doctoral research – Executive Gremlins or 'buttons' – and her current research on mindfulness at Oxford University. What we mean by these terms is described in detail in the coming chapters but in essence we deal with 'the little voices in the head' and how they hold you back, what is going on in the brain when these little voices are speaking. We show slides that illustrate the thoughts we had about each other when we first met.

FIGURE 3.5

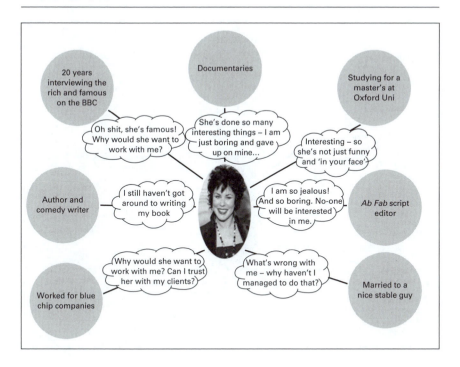

These were my first thoughts about Ruby. I was slightly in awe of her, to say the least. She has been interviewing the rich and famous for 20 years on TV. She is an author, editor and more. I felt intimidated. I also felt a little surprised that she had studied neuroscience and was studying for a master's degree in mindfulness at Oxford. I had been viewing her through my filters that she is funny, not that she is intelligent. I was to learn later that she hates it when strangers expect her to be funny and don't take her seriously. It all started to make me feel 'not good enough' and 'boring – no one will be interested in me'. When I share this with audiences, they aren't too surprised. We are all in awe of working with somebody famous, right? What is perhaps more surprising is what was going on in Ruby's head when she met me.

When Ruby met me she felt in awe of my qualifications and corporate experience. She also felt the same surprise that I had done a little

FIGURE 3.6

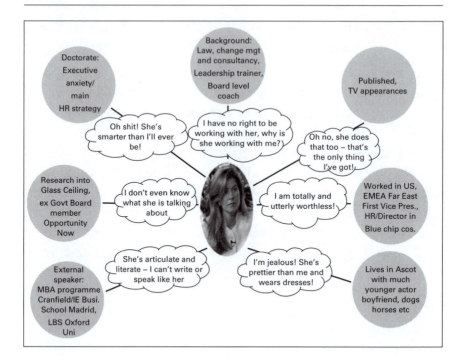

media work. It is interesting that we both registered a 'button push' when the other appeared to be stepping on our territory. (She usually makes the joke about never having heard of me, which is hardly surprising – it my media appearance wasn't exactly massive!) What also emerged was that she would normally have judged me for being 'a stiff in a suit'. It turns out that I reminded her of her mother, who dressed up, went to work and wore pearls – hardly the image I was going for! The audience does not generally expect Ruby to have any self-doubts, so this is usually a surprise.

I describe what gremlins are and how they manifest and how to identify and handle them – basically the information contained in this book. Ruby goes on to describe what is going on in the brain when these gremlins are active. She talks about negative emotions promoting the release of cortisol, which, she says:

> *shrinks the brain, causes brain cells to die, leads to disease and burnout, and makes you fat!*

She discusses how, when she did her TV show, her gremlins were active and all she was worried about was doing a good show:

> *I'd be leaning into the person, willing them to be interesting or funny but all I saw in their eyes was terror!*

She realized that her gremlins were making her 'attack' people. It was entertainment but not the sort of work she wanted to do. She is now doing amazing work with people suffering from depression following the success of her show *Losing it*. In corporate work she has a classic video clip of her and Madonna that she deconstructs. Madonna is feisty and unhelpful, which pushes Ruby's buttons and she attacks her right back. Before long they are both reacting to button pushes and neither is listening to the other. The body language clearly shows that they are not in rapport and Ruby discusses the self-limiting thoughts that were going on in her head. In other clips, with Imelda Marcos and Bette Midler she has them eating out of her hand as she skilfully encourages them to relax. With the latter, Bette is quite frosty at first but, after they share memories from their pasts and Bette recognizes that Ruby is 'real', she relaxes and they are soon talking like old friends. With Imelda, they got along so well she was invited to stay on for days after the interview finished. These are all classic examples of what goes on in even extremely talented and successful minds, especially in high-stress situations. This is true for people whether they are business executives or media celebrities, sportspeople or academics.

Anxious stressed-out executives do not make good leaders

People look for role models and mentors. We admire and respect people who 'have handled their stuff'. We want to know that it is possible to be successful and ultimately, most people who have made it want to give something back. If we allow ourselves to become stressed and anxious we will not make good leaders. In workshops when I ask the question 'Who are good leaders?' the same names always come up: Richard Branson, Nelson Mandela, Martin Luther King, Margaret Thatcher. All of these were at times flawed individuals yet they are held up as examples of great leaders. There are many reasons for this but one is that they are authentic and real and appear to be calm and in control. Contrast this with leaders held up as being poor (I will spare their blushes) and they tend to be lacking in interpersonal skills and manifest with negative behaviours and beliefs either about themselves or others. Leaders must recognize the effects of unconscious bias and look for contrary evidence. Once you are aware that 'your reality is not their reality', that it is just your brain seeking to find pattern matches from your past experiences, you will be able to recognize your gremlins, deal with them in the present and help your people to do the same.

In this chapter we have looked at perceptual filters and how they affect the way we perceive current situations. To help illustrate this, I described how Ruby Wax and I first viewed each other and which Executive Gremlins were activated. In the next chapter I will explain in detail how to deconstruct a challenging situation and work out both what gremlin was at work and also how to make new decisions in the moment.

The Executive Advantage 10-Step Solution for Resilient 21st-century Leaders©

A process for identifying and handling Executive Gremlins in the context of the organization

Most leaders are successful, fairly well-balanced individuals – aren't they? Well, yes and no! Whilst I would not say most successful leaders are running around stressed-out all the time, there are moments in everyone's careers where the pressure gets to us, where we judge ourselves and self-doubt. If we are really unlucky, it leads to burnout. If, as part of your development as a leader, you have studied this process and already know where your areas of sensitivity lie, you will be better equipped to deal with whatever hits you in this world of 21st-century leadership. In the same way that Olympic athletes train to compete in competition, and hone their muscles and techniques, you need to train ahead for the competitive world of organizations in the 21st century. You need to test and train your emotional muscle to be at your best. This process will give you the executive advantage you seek and make you a more resilient 21st-century leader.

We have explored what Executive Gremlins are and how they have operated in both my own life as a leader in business and in the lives of my clients. This process identifies how to 'surface' these gremlins and, in doing so, helps you to reframe and handle them in the context of your organization. It is possible to work through this process on your own and to learn more about yourself in the context of your organization. It is also, by its very nature, difficult to do objectively. Be as honest as possible with yourself. Do not edit this – you do not have to share what you find with anyone. This is not promoted as an alternative to executive coaching, psychotherapy or counselling that may be more appropriate solutions in some circumstances.

In working through the process yourself, take some quiet time in a place where you will not be disturbed. Let your mind wander in response to each stage but capture it on paper as you will not remember the detail later and you may need to revisit for clues. You may also want to reflect on these papers in a few months' time to see if a pattern is emerging. Different trigger events will be showing up the same gremlins. Knowing what your gremlins are is invaluable. With time and patience the process of identifying what is going on in any situation will happen almost immediately. Like driving a car, you will eventually get to the stage where you just *know* which gremlin has been activated and be able to make new decisions in the moment. Once you are clear about your own gremlins you may be able to venture – *very carefully* – into the wider world of other people's.

Handling Executive Gremlins in others is not a step-by-step process to be followed by the inexperienced, but is an iterative process where the coach or leader brings their skills and knowledge toolkit to the table and works with others, exploring executives' needs and fears by incisive questioning and listening. When they have identified what it is that is the cause of the problem, it is possible to identify ways of handling and coping with them. It may be necessary to revisit these steps over and over again before they get an insight or they may jump to it straight away, depending upon how strong the trigger is and how open or defended the person is. When you are confident and comfortable with handling your own gremlins you may be tempted to try it with others. My advice is: 'Don't!' This is known as attempting to handle someone else's case and is inappropriate and most leaders are not skilled enough to do this. Leaders are encouraged to obtain executive advantage training if they wish to use this process with their people.

The process is described in detail in Figures 4.1 and 4.2.

You should expect to spend a significant amount of time learning to work through your inner world. I suggest keeping a notebook and jotting down details of an upsetting situation immediately after it happens. Yes, I know, after such times the last thing we want to do is relive it. But if this was easy, everyone would be doing it! Athletes don't improve just by looking back at contests they won. You will not have to stay there long, just take a look. As soon as possible, go through the steps and identify a gremlin. You will start to see patterns and learn that different situations seem to activate the same areas of sensitivity. Eventually, identifying new gremlins will stop. You will realize that all your emotionally upsetting situations come down to some core gremlins and that these are the areas that you need to learn to live with and control in order to be happier and more effective. I run half-day to six-month programmes to help executives to do this. When I talk about 'handling your buttons' in presentations now, executives ask me where they can learn more about it. The result is this book. If you give it time, it will bring about a shift that will help you at all the levels in your life, personally and professionally, and ultimately your improved performance will impact on your organization's performance in a positive way.

When I am working with clients I always bear in mind that the 10-Step Solution is not always a sequential process and I judge when the moment is right to delve further or when to move on to the next step. It may be necessary to revisit steps if the individual is 'stuck' and unable to move on. Individuals may be resistant to change or afraid of the process itself. It is important to discern

FIGURE 4.1

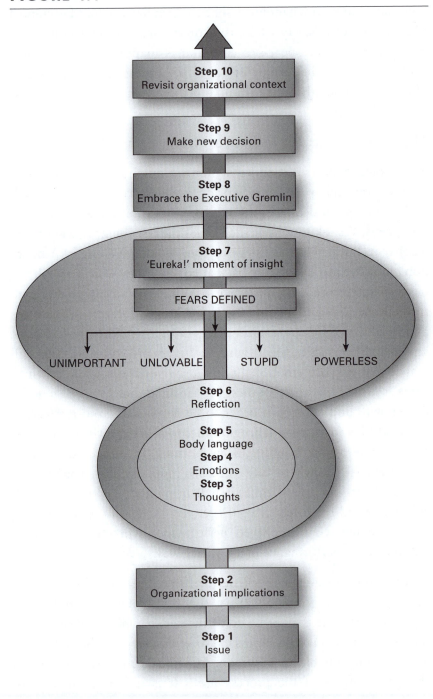

FIGURE 4.2

The Executive Advantage 10-Step Solution (working on your own Executive Gremlins)

1   **The presenting issue** – Identify the 'activating event' (run it out)

2   **Organizational context** – What is going on in the environment that may affect this situation?

3   **Thoughts** – List them (do not edit – be as graphic as possible)

4   **Emotions** – Associate an emotion with each thought; write this down too

5   **Body reactions** – Ask yourself if you experienced any; list them

6   **Personal Toolkit** – Keep reflecting back; reflect on words and observe

7   **Original outcome?** Identify for yourself and for the organization

8   **The 'clunk' moment** – When the moment of insight occurs you will feel it

9   **Embrace the fear** – Identify new ways of dealing with it and take actions; make new choices

10   **Revisit the organizational context** – What will you do differently and what will the likely consequences be?

---

the difference between the process not working and the individual being afraid of it working. If it is the latter, I go right back, build rapport and trust and explore further. It could be a very unhelpful process if someone starts to open up, hits an emotional block, and is then shut down because I lose their confidence in the process. Used well, it works. When you are working through this process alone it is important that you trust it and give it time. If feelings come up, just allow them, note them down and move on. Learning to do this is unbelievably valuable. It may take six months to learn about all your inner Executive Gremlins and how they manifest in your professional life, but once you have, you will find it improves your decision making and your performance. By default, it will also help your home life!

In the detailed explanation of the Solution which follows, I have made use of autobiography and case studies. I have used the same case study in more than one step to illustrate the process.

Step 1 – Identify an activating event

Write down what happened in the situation that has caused you stress.

Executives present with a wide variety of issues from their working and personal lives. Almost all relate to the 'little voice in the head' or the 'gremlin on the shoulder'. Even the most successful executives on the boards of major global corporations experience these crises of confidence at times. Most of these vulnerabilities arise when buttons are pressed. When this happens we overreact and our behaviour contributes to a negative outcome for ourselves, for others, or for the organization.

Most of my experiences in the past arose because I had the Executive Gremlins of 'Unlovable' and 'Unsafe' operating. I often found I had difficulties trusting the motivations of others and would get stressed by insensitive e-mails or silences, and start reading into them things that weren't actually there. An example of this would be when a colleague left one of my big corporate clients and joined me as a director in my company, which was operating very profitably. We subsequently had a less successful year and I was unable to give her the level of work she needed. She eventually decided to go it alone and left. We discussed our situation and agreed that we would still try to work together in the future. She then got involved with another group of people and we were then both seeking work with the client she used to work for. She said she would behave honourably and just wanted work but I found myself second-guessing, especially after I had offered her a small piece of work in the same organization and she responded by turning it down because she didn't want to 'feel compromised'. She also avoided meeting with me but still said on the phone that she wanted work through my company. I believed she was less emotionally driven than me and therefore did not feel the need for giving or receiving reassurances. I had no evidence that she was untrustworthy and yet I did not trust her. By utilizing the 10-Step Solution, I was able to identify what was causing my fear and by labelling it, I became calmer and more objective. We are still collaborating some eight years later!

CASE STUDY

She's short and chubby with 'big hair', a typical Irish stereotype. She is always in the middle of family dramas. She is head of IT and connects at all levels of the business from the chairman down. She communicates well with most people, she is empathetic but doesn't connect with me. When I have a meeting with her she comes in like a whirlwind and talks too fast. I feel overwhelmed and irritated when she takes things over without checking with me. Before meetings I feel 'ugh' and expect her to be late. She presents as scatty but actually does everything she is asked. Can you coach her? (Executive A; MD, global investment bank)

Executive A presented the issue of a difficult team member. Although I did indeed take this lady on as a client (and she did present exactly as described!), I was interested to see where my original client's behaviour was not helping and what Executive Gremlins of her own were adding to the situation. We used my process for explicating her fears and found it related to the fear of being 'Powerless'. For those familiar with Myers–Briggs Type Indicator (MBTI), Client A is borderline E/I on the Myers–Briggs profile introversion–extroversion dimension whilst her direct report was extreme extroversion with no ability to modify her behaviour to suit others. The fact that she worked well with client A's chairman and other board members contributed to client A's fear and feelings of being overwhelmed by both her personal style and her actions.

CASE STUDY

I felt all respect had been stripped away, and hated the sympathy it evoked in others. It knocked my self-confidence and I felt a bit sick and flushed.

(Executive B; programme director for large telecoms company)

This was the aforementioned very senior director of a large global telecoms company running £ billion government projects. He had been at a conference where the CEO had completely put him down in public, in front of 2,000 people.

Whilst my client knew the CEO did not think badly of him, in the moment it was a big blow for this normally confident individual. We explored and worked through this event using my process and we identified that there were two Executive Gremlins in operation, 'Weak' and 'Unlovable'. Weak because he was unable to defend himself in the situation and Unlovable because someone he had previously looked up to apparently thought so little of him. Whilst we both knew that the CEO in question was often described as a bully, we discussed his reaction and concluded that it was probably stronger than someone who did not have these particular fears would have been, as illustrated in Figure 4.3.

Response to external stimuli

FIGURE 4.3

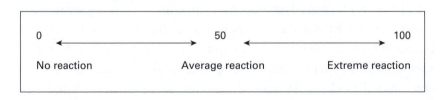

A person full of confidence and in balance would have seen the external stimulus for what it was – a rather inadequate person with lots of executive fears using inappropriate language and putting others down. They would have little or no reaction. A person with mild Executive Gremlins would probably have had some reaction to this event as everyone likes positive reinforcement and very few people respond well to put-downs. Finally, a person with an Unlovable process, who is very focused on what others think of them and who also feels weak in the presence of (perceived) more powerful individuals like the CEO, would have an extreme reaction to such a stimulus, to the point of feeling sick (fear), and flushed (anger). Anger is a common emotion that arises around feeling weak. As it was inappropriate to show it verbally in this environment, his body reacted instead.

When coaching leaders and undertaking step 1, I listen carefully to what they are saying and listen actively for an event to be raised and what to question more closely about. Key words will give away the fact that there is an emotional attachment and these may be fed back and further questions asked. Judgement is used to decide whether to press for further details or to leave this one for a future meeting. At this stage I am assessing whether to be supportive or more challenging, whether to 'push' or 'pull'. In my experience it is easier to push and be more challenging once a robust relationship has developed. When working on your own you will need to consider all aspects, pushing yourself beyond your comfort zones to find new answers and delving deep to find new meanings. You will need to make notes of your perception of the situation.

I went through a very difficult time in my late 30s and early 40s. I lost a full-term baby at birth through hospital negligence and then my partner left me and moved in with a 23-year-old. He continued to see us both, and I became pregnant and lost two more babies through miscarriage the following year. Though a normally strong person, my self-esteem was at an all-time low and my 'Unlovable', 'Unattractive' and 'Unsafe' fears were really controlling my external world. I remember a particular morning when I was due to deliver a top team workshop for an IT company and I just panicked. I felt that I simply couldn't do it. All I could think about was how heartbroken I was and I was desperately in need of support. I called my ex from my mobile phone and he said 'Well, what do you want me to do about it?' I remember shaking and crying and not knowing what to do. However, it did help me because it made me angry enough to do something different. I made the decision not to let my Executive Gremlins control me. I took myself away, 'centred' myself and got on with the job. I did a short mental exercise to focus my mind on reality rather than fear. I made a different decision because I was conscious of the fact that my fears weren't real but rather a projection of my low self-esteem at the time. In doing so, I created new neural connections in my brain which ultimately helped me to form more helpful beliefs. Often just knowing that the fears are active is enough to allow a different choice in the moment as the limbic system calms down. I am sure it wasn't my best performance but I got through it and did not let my fears control me.

I sometimes teach the following short mental exercise in workshops that just involves sitting down somewhere and focusing on each area of your body:

- Tense and relax the muscles slightly to become aware of them and work down from the top of your head to your toes.

- Deliberately focus on your breathing. Slow your breathing and breathe from your belly.

- Focus on where your body is touching the seat, where there is pressure, where you are holding tension, and deliberately relax each part.

- Become aware of your feet on the floor, imagine all the tension in your body flowing out of your feet into the floor.

- When you experience a 'button push' you will find this extremely difficult to focus on but with practice it works and the act of doing it calms your mind.

Another is when you are aware you feel under threat to imagine a large bell jar coming down over you. As it descends, imagine some music playing that makes you feel powerful (mine is the *Mission: Impossible* theme tune!). When the bell jar is in place, see arrows and darts coming at you but simply bouncing off the bell jar. Focus on feeling powerful and energized. Remember, the brain doesn't know the difference between suggestion and reality!

If all this sounds crazy, feel free not to do it but it helps some people when they are aware they are not thinking straight and feeling emotional. An Olympic diver I coached found these exercises very effective before competitions. He achieved Commonwealth Silver and substantial lottery funding for his Olympics training.

Whilst you are primarily involved with thinking about your world at work, you may become aware of issues relating to your personal life. This may be a time to seek out expert help (eg drug or alcohol abuse counselling). Sometimes relationship issues mirror those at work. Mostly, anything that is affecting your personal life will be having an impact on your professional life as well and vice versa. This is because you will be in a state of 'activation' – the unhelpful emotional state which will affect your ability to think clearly.

Step 2 – Think about the organizational context; make notes

This is important for two reasons: first and obviously because the impact on the organization has to be considered, and second to enable you to focus on your anxiety and how your choices and behaviour that stem from it impact on the outside world. Without this context, this process could stray into the world of psychotherapy or life coaching. When working with clients it is my experience and background in organizations that make this approach unique.

When we work together, I am able to help my clients because I understand their perspectives as directors in global businesses. I am able to use my background of running my own businesses and of working at board level to bring rationality to the discussion, to discuss organizational politics and how to influence within an organization. An experienced leader in any organization who is able to deconstruct a difficult often political argument, whilst 'owning their own part' (ie 'What did I do in this situation that wasn't helpful?') will have an inherent executive advantage and be a more authentic 21st-century leader.

Step 3 – List all thoughts

Write down all your thoughts – about the issue, about yourself, and the thoughts you had about the other parties involved.

Listing the thoughts an individual has about a situation is really an exercise in running out judgements based on the perceptual lenses through which you see the world. This exercise helps you to 'own' these judgements and also gives you pointers about your fears. You sometimes even use the language of the Executive Gremlins at work, eg 'I felt unimportant or weak.' It is important to own these judgements when doing this for yourself. Don't edit what you really thought. Do not place any significance on any single thought at this stage. Underline any words that immediately bring to mind a gremlin, eg 'Disregarded', 'Unimportant', 'Powerless'. You will return to these later.

As an executive coach it is important that I build a strong enough relationship with the individual to make them feel I am a safe space to share. Some of the thoughts people have are very politically in-correct and involve swearing and other things they would not usually share with others – especially if their fears included things that lead to being 'appropriate'. I introduce this step as 'Down and dirty – give it to me warts and all,' and they will if they trust me. Without trust and rapport it will not happen at the required depth. I ask them to write their thoughts down. I have found the process of writing their judgements down helps them own them. It also often raises inappro-priate judgements to their conscious minds and is an opportunity to discuss them and any unhelpful pre-existing filters or unconscious bias. I do not place any significance on any single thought over another at this stage.

Step 4 – Associate an emotion with each thought

Write them down in a list beside each thought.

Much has been written about emotions. Interestingly, what we think about tends to drive how we feel. Identifying the emotions helps in the explication process as you will begin to recognize that you have a choice, that what you choose to believe and think drives how you feel and behave. This awareness helps reduce the control the Executive Gremlin has over you and helps individuals to *respond* to situations rather than *react* to them.

Executive A

In the example given above in Step 1 we discussed Executive A's 'annoying' new direct report. When I asked her to list all her thoughts, Table 4.1 is what she came up with.

TABLE 4.1

Thought	Emotion/feeling
She's late	Anger
OK, she's not late	Anger
She's a flouncy mess	Anger
She talks at 90 mph	Very angry
She's just deflecting my questions	Anger
She won't let me in	Sadness
She doesn't listen	Anger
She doesn't take my point of view on board	Weakness
She doesn't respect me	Anger
She doesn't give me the attention I deserve	Sadness
Have I intimidated her?	Guilt
Was I too sharp previously?	Guilt
Has she recovered from it?	Guilt
I feel bombarded	Anger
I feel overwhelmed/can't cope	Weakness
I feel ineffectual	Weakness
I feel let down	Sadness

The process of listing these thoughts and emotions clearly shows how my client moved through her initial feelings of anger and disgust (emotions she projected *at* the other party) to thoughts, feelings and emotions about herself. By the end she was feeling guilty, weak and sad. It became clear that she had a pattern of first blaming others in a situation and then turning these negative feelings and emotions on herself. The words she used gave me clues to help her discover which Executive Gremlins were activated by this person.

Write down an emotion for each thought even if it is the same one. Sometimes you may feel that it is all the same emotion at the beginning but then about halfway through, it may change. Hence this client experienced angry feelings towards the other party and then about halfway through realized that the anger had turned inwards and she blamed herself. This is where the Executive Gremlin has taken over, even though at this stage they may not know which one has been activated. By discussing this they often use words that reflect their fear, eg 'I felt completely powerless/stupid.' I make a mental note at this stage to come back to this.

Step 5 – Did you experience any physical reactions?

If so, write them down.

I have experienced a pain in my chest: when my brother died, when I lost my child at birth and also when my relationship ended shortly afterwards. I have also felt a tension in my stomach. Body reactions are not experienced by everyone. However, they do provide additional clues to how you are feeling.

In the description of Executive B above, we examined how he felt about being put down by his CEO in public. He said he felt 'slightly sick and flushed'. Sickness is often associated with extreme fear (which we discovered in his case were the fears of being Weak and Unlovable) and 'flushed' suggests he was angry and his body was giving away his desire to fight.

As we have seen, this is because the body was originally programmed to run away from stressful situations – the 'flight or fight' response from early days identified in the 19th century by physiologist Walter Cannon, Professor of Medicine at Harvard Medical School. However, that response was probably originally intended to respond to physical danger, such as a dangerous animal, by equipping us to run away – to survive. The modern executive faces the *same level of reaction* to situations that are perceived as dangerous even if they are mental or emotional rather than physical. Our bodies become physically stronger and quicker, our blood leaves our hands and feet and we feel cold. Adrenaline and noradrenaline are released into the bloodstream, accelerating the heart rate and increasing oxygen consumption. All this physical response shows itself in cold sweaty handshakes, shaking when presenting, or an inability to think straight in the boardroom when faced with hostile non-executive directors. The executive can therefore be in a physical state of terror under the surface whilst trying to appear calm and reasonable to the outside world.

I ask executives if they experienced any physical reactions: for example, heat is often reported as reflecting anger, cold as reflecting fear; a knot in the solar plexus often reflects repressed emotion, pain in the heart area, when someone is suffering extreme sadness – for example when dealing with the death of a loved one. I learned to recognize body reactions when I trained as a breath-work practitioner (a therapeutic intervention). They are also reported by executive clients now when they describe their experiences in the boardroom, eg 'I was boiling mad,' 'I felt my blood run cold,' 'I was shaking with anger.'

Step 6 – Reflection; ask yourself deeper questions

Make a note of your thoughts.

This is the stage where you need to delve deeper. It will be challenging but possible to do this alone. Review what you have already written down and ask yourself where you have experienced this feeling before; what does it remind you of? The patterns will start to emerge. Challenge yourself to think outside the box. Ask yourself what sort of person would have done what you did as though you are a third party. Your judgements of yourself give vital clues. Review what you have identified so far as if you were reviewing a business plan. Where are the holes and the flaws? Keep going with this even if it feels tough. Maybe go for a walk, let your mind dwell on it. Don't try too hard, though – this may be counterproductive!

Mining questions are the sort of questions that take people deeper than just a first-level question which elicits a fairly superficial response. You will need to ask yourself some mining questions.

I use a wide range of 'personal toolkit' skills and knowledge to elicit more information when coaching. It is essential that the coach or leader attempting to use this with anyone other than themselves has a robust and varied personal toolkit. For example, mine include:

- Corporate experience and knowledge (I have small and large company experience and in the commercial and government sectors).

- Law, HR strategy and board-level experience.

- Primal therapy and breathwork.

- Drugs, alcohol and other types of abuse counselling.

- General counselling, bereavement counselling.

- Performance coaching, neuroleadership and coach training.

- Mentoring.

- Visualization techniques.

- Neuroscience and mindfulness.
- Research.
- An interest in health and fitness.
- Personal experiences with maternity and motherhood.
- Being a senior woman in a male-dominated environment.

I have utilized my entire personal toolkit in leadership roles in organizations. If you have reached an executive-level role in any significant organization you will have your own, equally useful personal toolkit. Whatever yours comprises, use it to ask yourself questions you would not normally ask.

Step 7 – Explore the original outcome

How could you modify your behaviour to elicit a different/better outcome?

Focusing on outcomes allows you to see the consequences of allowing your limiting self-beliefs and Executive Gremlins to control you. It is important at this stage to review carefully what the perceived outcome was and to question yourself about your behaviour at the time. Consider alternative outcomes and what behaviours you would need to adopt. Clarify exactly what happened. Once you have achieved clarity about the present situation, you are able to envision a more positive future.

CASE STUDY   Executive A

Returning to Executive A with the 'annoying' direct report, we are able to see that the original outcome of their meeting resulted in her feeling angry and disgusted, being more formal than she normally was and trying to avoid her subordinate. By working through and gaining clarity about what was actually going on we were able to see that she could get a better outcome by adopting a more friendly approach. I suggested she took the other woman to lunch and allowed her to calm down (she was clearly demonstrating needy behaviour and seemed to be trying too hard to prove herself). I also suggested that she confronted how she felt in meetings with her subordinate and admitted to feeling overwhelmed in her presence. By showing her own vulnerabilities she came across as more human to her subordinate who in return disclosed that she too felt uncomfortable and wanted to do something about her unhelpful behaviour.

It is important to describe the outcome in detail and to consider all possible outcomes. At this stage the process is purely descriptive. How could you have modified your behaviour to elicit a different one? Think outside the box.

Step 8 – Insight; the 'eureka!' moment

Naming the Executive Gremlin – write it down; see if it resonates.

At this stage you may feel you have explored enough to be able to ask yourself what you think the executive fear may be. It may be helpful initially to review what executive fears are and how they operate, to name some.

Executive Gremlins:

- Unimportant;
- Weak;
- Powerless;
- Not good enough;
- Unlovable;
- Disregarded;
- Fat, Ugly;
- Stupid;
- Out of control.

People are more inclined to share with, or open up to, a fellow human, not someone who looks down from on high. It's all about creating a safe environment.

Depending on what the individual has presented with, I may choose to share a fear or button that I think has relevance to them. For instance, if they have been talking about thoughts to do with being disregarded or ignored I may talk about my Unlovable process; if they talk about being respected then I would focus on my Unimportant process. If I think they may have a 'Stupid' fear, which I don't have, I will describe it in generic terms, saying 'I don't really have a Stupid fear but if I did I would likely be worried about xyz.' I leave them to make the connections with their own behaviours and fears. This is one of the ways my work diverges from that of other coaches.

CASE STUDY   Executive A and her subordinate

In a meeting with Executive A's subordinate, she told me that she was not a graduate and had always worried about that. Also, she felt she was not good enough compared to other people she worked with. She was not rich and lived a fairly ordinary life and was not glamorous like a lot of the VPs with whom she worked. She also mentioned that she feared presenting. 'I hate it although I am told I am OK at it.' I remembered a time when I had felt the same and told her about my experience and how I had overcome it. I also talked about my 'Unimportant' and 'Not good enough' fears. The more I was willing to be fallible the more she told me, the more connections she made to her own fears. Executive A identified a 'Powerless' fear as a result of the process involving this subordinate. Whilst some of Executive A's observations of her subordinate had been accurate from the outset, she did not know what was driving this from her subordinate's internal world and she did not enjoy the emotions that she (Executive A) felt every time she dealt with her. When Executive A changed her own behaviour (by taking her subordinate to lunch and spending time with her) she helped her subordinate to address her unhelpful behaviours too. Changing behaviour in this way is also an example of Step 9, 'Embracing the Gremlin', below.

Replaying words back to yourself that you have used earlier in the process – eg 'I felt hopeless/powerless' – will often indicate a gremlin, in this case a 'Powerless' or 'Weak' fear.

The 'eureka!' moment – creating insight

This moment happens when you identify the underlying Executive Gremlin operating in the presenting issue. It can be very distinct, even dramatic, as realization dawns. It is often referred to as 'the light-bulb moment' as things fall into place. It is essential that you reserve judgement until this moment and it takes skill to judge when it has happened or is about to happen. The 'eureka!' moment may come very quickly or be a very protracted drawn-out process, depending on the strength of the trigger and how 'defended' you are. Also, as you become familiar with your core needs and gremlins, you will start to make quicker connections to them and begin to better understand your limiting self-beliefs.

> When I started using this process to identify my own fears, it took me a long time to work out what was going on and I often needed help with the process. As I became familiar with my core fears, I realized that these underpinned many of my stressful situations.

CASE STUDY   Executive C

This client is a senior partner of a major law firm. He is extremely well known and powerful in the City. He arrived with a fear of presenting, despite the fact that presenting is a necessary part of his job. He confessed that he avoided making presentations and, if he was forced to, he dreaded them. He is also published in another field and was due to make a big presentation at an opening of his work in a prestigious location in London. He had increased the pressure on himself by inviting a lot of his City colleagues to the opening. He is from Hong Kong originally and worries that his language skills will not be good enough and that he will say the wrong thing or use language inappropriately. Explicating his fears was extremely difficult as he was very defended and resisted admitting any weakness whatsoever. He had recently gone through a messy divorce and was very angry and upset but he could not articulate this. I worked with him for about a month before his big presentation and the breakthrough came at, and after, his opening. When I saw his work I raised the possibility that the metaphor that might work for him was that of his creative work. By exploring his fears and feelings through his work we were able to identify his 'Not good enough' and 'Stupid' fears and then to apply these back into the world of global markets and law. He is still a complicated character but we are making progress.

The human brain is an information-processing system, it executes routine physical tasks but struggles at times with mental tasks. It works out logical solutions to problems using what is known as 'working memory'. We use our working memory to make decisions when we don't have an obvious answer to problems. It is used for cognitive tasks. However, it has limited capacity. Take mental arithmetic: most people find adding simple numbers reasonably easy but we have to work harder as the numbers increase in size. The brain maxes out. Yet other parts of our brain are performing much more complex 'non-conscious' tasks all the time, eg standing up or sitting down. Herein lies the problem. Most leadership decisions nowadays require too much working memory as they have no pre-existing logic. Solutions tend to happen when you are doing something else, like sleeping, walking, gardening, exercising. New research tells us how to increase the likelihood of having more 'eureka!' moments. David Rock has identified the following conditions for creating insights:

- *Quiet* – insights tend to involve connections between small numbers of neurons – we need quiet to 'hear' them or they get lost in the noise.
- *Inward looking* – mind wandering is good for insights; external focus on a problem is not.
- *Slightly happy* – as opposed to slightly anxious – helps people solve more problems and be more creative.

- *Not effortful* – stop trying to solve the problem! Wrong solutions tend to push out correct ones and we keep focusing on the wrong one. Creativity is stifled.

This stage is very difficult to describe in words but much easier in practice. You can't force an 'aha!' or 'eureka!' moment but you can put your brain into a receptive state by free association and relaxation. It is very important when doing the 10-Step Solution that you give yourself space for this. You may need to wander around a park, play some squash, go and have lunch, before an insight occurs – but it will. Having insights is actually fun and positive if you don't judge yourself. It gives the brain a boost of dopamine – the happy drug! Years of working with this approach have helped me to identify when this intuitive moment occurs. When you find it you will think 'That's it, that's the one!' with some emotion. I do not lead my clients to their solution and as a leader going through this process you should not try to guess! You will know when you have found it because you will 'feel' it.

Step 9 – Embracing the gremlin

Write down what you are going to do – commit to it.

This stage is about taking the fear and confronting it head on. It is where individuals are encouraged to put themselves in situations that are likely to activate the gremlin and to deal with the emotions this brings up. Usually, the actual experience is less painful than the fear of the experience: 'The pain is in the resistance' (Rob Rider).

CASE STUDY   Executive A

Let's return to Executive A's 'annoying' subordinate once again. When she took her subordinate to lunch she was 'embracing the fear' because she did not want to do it and she knew she would have to control her anger and disgust in order to change the dynamic between them. In doing so she risked activating her 'Powerless' gremlin that we had identified was the one activated by her relationship with this woman. We also deliberately looked for opportunities for her to put herself in situations where she would feel powerless and out of her comfort zone (like a TV interview on a subject she wasn't completely comfortable with) to help her realize that the reality is that she was an extremely powerful and influential executive of a major City institution.

'Embracing the gremlin' involves the executive agreeing to take actions to 'shrink' the size and impact of the Executive Gremlin. This may be quite challenging and actions that to one person without the particular gremlin would be quite easy may seem insurmountable to someone in fear. For example, an experienced, extroverted thinking leader would not be fazed by speaking at a top talent forum, with 2,000 people attending, but it would be a horrendous experience for an introverted feeler with a 'Stupid' gremlin. If you are trying to set an action for yourself, think of the opposite to what you would choose to do. For example, if you think you have an Important need, put yourself in a situation where you are a nobody, do not talk about your achievements, leave the big car and the designer labels at home. Observe the reactions of those around you. If you think you have a need to be liked, go to a couple of meetings and refrain from small talk, don't worry about others, maybe be blunt and direct on a topic without worrying about how it lands. See if anyone notices; chances are they won't. If you suffer from feeling weak and powerless at times, surround yourself with the types who make you feel that way and just be with the feelings it evokes, don't fight it, just let it come up and pass. What you will find is that no one notices! If you fear looking stupid, try presenting to large audiences, or write a paper on something that you have researched. Challenge yourself to confront looking stupid. One extreme exercise I do on leadership retreats is to get people to shout at traffic: 'Your disapproval makes me laugh.' If you are cringing at the very thought now, ask yourself 'Why?' Is it inappropriate or out of control? Think about your reaction. The vast majority of people around you would find it amusing or don't notice. It's amazingly freeing. We are all so wrapped up in ourselves that we barely notice what strangers are up to. Once you realize this it becomes easier to try out more sensible things, confident that you are not being judged by the world around you all the time.

FIGURE 4.4

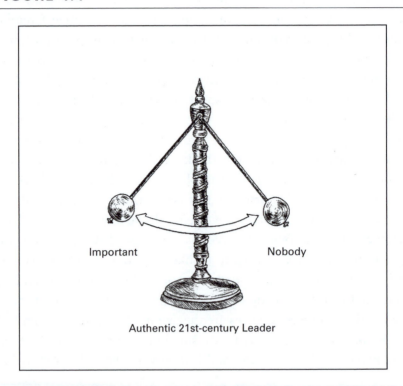

Important   Nobody

Authentic 21st-century Leader

Remember the pendulum I described earlier about conflict? Imagine one now. On the left is your normal behaviour, say being a big important business person with all the trappings of success. On the right is being a nobody, with nothing. By swinging over to the other side you are able to come back to a more balanced place, in the middle. You are able to feel successful and important without needing it so much that it actively derails your performance.

Step 10 – Revisit the organizational context

What will you do differently? Write it down and commit to actions. Make them tangible with measures and dates for completion.

It is perhaps in step 10 that we overcome the 'So what?' test. What makes this approach unique is that we are dealing with executives' individual inner worlds and fears *in the context of their outer world, the organization.* It is also where we test that you are truly ready to deal with the gremlin as it may threaten your fundamental belief systems. The brain does not enjoy change. It looks for patterns to make sense of your world. Taking new actions will form new habits, which will in turn create new mental pathways. This is where your change in perception and behaviour really starts to create a change in performance that positively benefits the organization and creates an executive advantage.

I help clients to reflect upon their reactions and hypersensitivity to activating situations and how this at least contributes to the problem – even when the other party is 99 per cent responsible for the conflict or issue, we still have a part, even if it is just making the choice whether to participate in the situation.

Many years ago, I was invited by a documentary producer (I will call him Matt) to get involved in a film travel company. He knew a woman (I will call her Mary) who had been organizing travel for major Hollywood stars for about 20 years. She was unhappy working with her existing partner and wanted to start up on her own. Neither had any idea how to set up a company and had no credibility with banks, nor could they get the licence to book flights direct (ABTA) until they had traded for a year. I agreed to help them and we agreed to a joint shareholding of 33.3 per cent each. We further agreed that only Mary would take a salary for the first couple of years until we had established enough cash flow for us all to benefit as both of us had other work and were not expecting to work full time in the business. This was because it is a low-margin business and we could not afford it. Matt and I had our own businesses outside this one. Mine was successful, but unfortunately Matt's existing business was in trouble; he was facing bankruptcy and moving out of his editing suite and office at a film studios. I negotiated deals with the bank and with factoring companies and with a travel company to act as our agent until we could get our licence. Matt did nothing, drew money out which wasn't there, bought himself suits, paid for his other business expenses and took his children out to dinners – all on the business. His behaviour meant we were trading insolvently and almost sent the company under. Unfortunately, Mary couldn't see it and would not listen to me. She said she 'didn't understand business' and said one thing to me in private – 'What can I do?' – and another to me when he was there – 'I don't mind'! He totally dominated and manipulated her. The more I challenged his dishonest behaviour the less she trusted me. As I was the only director with any money, and we were jointly and severally liable, I realized I would be the one the banks came to if the business went down. I couldn't see my way through and, after two years of trying, I resigned as director and returned my shares. I eventually identified that it was my Unlovable gremlin that was keeping me there. I wanted Mary to acknowledge my contribution and to believe me and she just didn't. She had formed a romantic attachment to Matt (who in my perception took advantage of it). Mary's pattern of allowing herself to be manipulated by men meant her filters were too strong to see the truth before her.

Thus, whilst I perceived that the problems in the business were 99 per cent 'his fault', I learned that it was my choice to stay in this emotionally damaging situation. Once I had identified the gremlin I was free to make new choices and to leave the business. I was able to look at how this situation was affecting my main business and to refocus my energies there.

The Executive Advantage 10-Step Solution

1. The presenting issue. Identify the 'activating event' (run it out).

2. Organizational context. What is going on in the environment that may affect this situation?

3. Thoughts. List them (do not edit – be as graphic as possible).

4. Emotions. Associate an emotion with each thought.

5. Body reactions. Ask yourself if you experienced any – list them.

6. Personal toolkit. Keep reflecting back – reflect on words and observe.

7. Original outcome? Identify for yourself and for the organization.

8. The 'clunk' moment. When the moment of insight occurs you will feel it.

9. Embrace the gremlin. Identify new ways of dealing with it and take actions – make new choices.

10. Revisit the organizational context. What will you do differently and what will the likely consequences be?

Actions

- Read this chapter carefully and proceed with caution. You may be surprised at the emotional response.

- Consider coaching or training in the methodology if you wish to use the methodology with your teams or clients (**www.transition-coaching.co.uk**).

In this chapter we have shown The Executive Advantage 10-Step Solution for Resilient 21st-century Leaders© and how you can use it to discover what your Executive Gremlins are and make better decisions in the moment in your organization. In the next chapter I explain how this works from a neuroleadership perspective and what is going on in your brain.

Neuroleadership and the 10-Step Solution

The thing about the brain is, it's complicated. Neuroscience is important to this book as it explains what is going on in our heads when we are experiencing 'brain overload' as a result of anxiety. This chapter provides a simple overview of current thinking. Neuroscience is basically the scientific study of the nervous system and is seen as a branch of biological sciences. However, in recent years many associated fields have come together with common interest including cognitive behavioural therapy (CBT), human givens psychotherapy, medicine, statistics and more. I have drawn heavily on the work of Dr David Rock, whom I work with in organizations in Europe and the USA, and who first used the term 'neuroleadership'. He has written several books on the subject. David describes neuroleadership as 'the application of findings from neuroscience to the field of leadership'. I also reference the work of Dr Anne Moir, a neuroscientist, for her work and research on neuroscience and gender. I have explored this subject here as there are significant differences in the male and female brains. The impact of neuroscience on developing resilient 21st-century leaders is that we finally have answers for *why* we feel the way we do when we experience a threat response when we are under stress and can work out helpful strategies for changing our behaviour and improve our decision making at work when going through change.

The evolution of brain development

The brain's development started millions of years ago in the course of evolution. There were three distinct phases:

- *Reptilian*, the oldest part of the brain includes the brain stem, which controls digestion, breathing and heartbeat. It is responsible for basic emotions such as hunger, fear, excitement, pleasure and anger. Reptilian brains were not developed enough to love and care for offspring properly, eg against predators.

- *Mammalian*, now known as the limbic system, was created as the first mammals were created. This is the area of the brain's nervous centre where the hippocampus and the amygdala are located. These are the parts of the brain which are responsible for storing memories. The resulting increased emotional ability allowed mammals to care for offspring and live within herds or packs, or even with partners.

- *Human*. The neocorticol brain was created millions of years ago. The cerebral cortex was greatly enhanced and allowed for the human species to plan, learn, adapt and communicate efficiently, and also to demonstrate empathetic and altruistic characteristics.

So what is going on in our heads now?

The limbic system (which includes the hippocampus and amygdala – the brain's fear circuitry) drives the rational frontal cortex of the brain. It is the older part where we experience pain, pleasure, fear and desire – the emotional part of the brain that also accesses long-term (emotional) memory. Jeffrey Schwartz, a world expert on obsessive-compulsive disorder says that 'brains are built to detect changes in the environment and send out strong signals to alert us to anything unusual'. This is why handling change at a personal and organizational level is so complex and threatening.

FIGURE 5.1

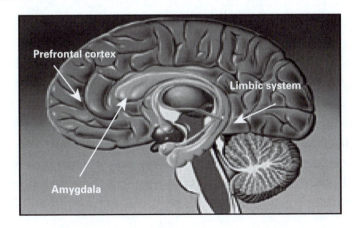

The prefrontal cortex is where intellect lives. It is the area we use when we undertake complex planning, decision making and moderating social behaviour. Its activities relate to goals, thoughts and actions. It has limited resources and can become fatigued, overwhelmed and overloaded by high levels of stress, or too much information, when our fear-based animal instincts start to take over. This is why, when we are experiencing high levels of change, we react emotionally and uncertainly and we may be unable to think rationally. In applying this to my research, I realized that many coaches when undertaking executive coaching tend to work mainly with the prefrontal cortex, on goals, strategies and actions. In fact they are trained to do this. Only focus on the positives! However, there will always be times when clients will be facing challenging situations or their brains are overloaded. It is normal. The 10-Step Solution really comes into play when Executive Gremlins have caused our limbic system to take over, when emotions are 'running riot' and the amygdala has reacted with a threat response – that is, the times when we can't control our responses. A typical example might be when a busy leader is threatened in some way and becomes stressed. By tackling this early, it is possible to stop burnout before it occurs. The mere act of *identifying*

a gremlin can calm the limbic system so that the threat response diminishes. Does it really matter that the brain cannot tell the difference between physical pain and emotional/social pain? The paper, 'The pains and pleasures of social life: a social cognitive neuroscience approach' (Eisenberger and Lieberman, 2009) showed that the same parts of the brain are activated by social distress as by physical pain symptoms. For instance, the more emotionally rejected a person feels, the stronger the pain response registered in the brain. The authors state that 'the brain is a social organ', that mammals need to be socially connected for survival, and that people experience work as a social system. Being asked to take a pay cut or being reprimanded may provoke a neural impulse as powerful and painful as a blow to the head. They believe that 'the ability to intentionally address the social brain in the service of optimal performance will be a distinguishing leadership capability in the years ahead'. They also report that whilst people can report how they feel, they are poor at reporting the reasons why they feel a certain way. The Executive Advantage 10-Step Solution helps them find those reasons and make new choices. As the brain doesn't know the difference between reality and fiction, a new idea or choice may stop the *reaction* to a given stimulus and provide more helpful strategies for success. If enough leaders start to behave in this way when going through complex change, a culture shift will occur. Stress will no longer be the hidden corporate *disease* as leaders will have coping mechanisms.

David Rock talks about the critical thread of research on the social brain which starts with the 'threat and reward' response. Evian Gordon refers to this as the 'minimize danger, maximize reward' response and calls it 'the fundamental organizing principle of the brain'. Neurons activate and hormones release as we learn whether a new person or situation is friend or foe. Researchers have also discovered that threat responses are more intense and longer lasting than reward responses. The impact of this shows up in organizations. When leaders are stressed, employees' brains become less efficient. When the leader helps people feel good about themselves, and communicates clearly their expectations, their people make better decisions and stronger relationships throughout periods of change.

Some other terms that you may hear include:

- *Hardwiring*, which is largely concerned with learned behaviour or beliefs – sometimes called 'neural pathways in the brain' or things we already 'know'.

- *Arousal*, which to neuroscientists is the physiological and psychological state of being awake, though the term is often used more widely to describe physical arousal in a sexual sense.

- *Working memory*, which involves the temporary storage and use of memory and for learning new activities. It operates extremely well if what we are doing is habitual routine activity.

- *Neuroplasticity*, which refers to the physiological changes that occur in the brain as a result of our experience. Research has shown that where we focus our attention is where we make new connections, so focusing our people's attention on new positive outcomes will create new neural connections and ultimately new behaviours. The executive advantage model helps people to pinpoint the underlying fear and make new more helpful choices in the moment. As we saw in Chapter 4, reviewing what we have learned about ourselves in the context of our organization, and deciding upon new actions, *will* build new habits and ultimately new neural pathways in our brains.

This validates the theory that 21st-century leadership development programmes should include experiential learning, such as project placements that involve actually applying theory back at work, interspersed with theory, and supported by executive coaching, rather than lots of new data alone. I have done this in many organizations but remember a particularly successful IT change programme where the company in question had won huge government projects. They were aware that they did not have enough leaders to lead on all aspects of the projects but did not want to pull in too many people from outside. We developed a 'supra competency' framework, measured their aspiring leaders against them, and developed a programme to address the gaps. We provided coaching between group sessions and the 'top talent' individuals were given 'stretch assignments' to learn on the job and test the theory learned on the course.

It is also why when managing ourselves or when leading and coaching people, we should act upon insights as soon as we see them. Sometimes it will be necessary to take a situation or an insight away and think more about it, to use the 10-Step Solution to break it down and to identify what is going on. At other times the insight is so immediate and so strong that the resilient leader will just know how to proceed. The more the leader 'runs the process' the faster they will get to insight and action. New neural pathways will be created and old patterns will be familiar. The brain is only able to take on a limited number of ideas and keep them in mind at any one time. Taking actions forms habits which embed new learning and create new, often more helpful pathways in the brain. An example of a learned behaviour would be learning to drive a car. At first it is an unconscious inability to drive – we don't know what we don't know. Then we have lessons and have to think and try to do it. We become consciously incompetent – we know we don't know how to do it! After a few lessons and lots of practice, most of us are consciously competent – we can drive but we have to think about it. We are still creating new connections and pathways. Finally, when we have passed our test and driven for a while we become unconsciously competent – we just drove home from work thinking about anything other than driving. It has become hardwired.

Learning to make new pathways is much harder work than following old ones. Similarly, change management requires people to do things differently and we don't like it! Whether it is changing how we communicate, how we sell, or how we lead others through it, many of us resist change simply because it is different and it is hard work for our brains! It is also why it is important to allow people to come to their own conclusions rather than to impose change on them and why a 'solutions focused' approach tends to work better than dwelling on a problem.

Finally, we come to hormones and neurotransmitters, which play a very important part in the study of neuroleadership. You have probably heard of 'fight or flight' theory (mentioned earlier in this book) in relation to stress. Basically, the theory is that we were programmed in the days of cavemen to recognize threats in the form of wild animals and to run away. There is a release of adrenaline and noradrenaline which increase heart rate, boosts the supply of oxygen and glucose to the brain and muscles, while suppressing other non-emergency processes, eg digestion. Now we no longer have to run away from sabre-toothed tigers, but we still have the same responses to perceived threats. This is why, when we fear a big presentation or meeting with the board, our hands shake, we sweat, our mouths go dry. Our bodies are preparing to run away! Conversely, dopamine is commonly associated with the pleasure system of the brain, providing positive feelings and reinforcement to motivate people to perform certain activities (which is why engagement and recognition work in organizations). Serotonin plays an important part in regulating mood, anger, sleep, sexuality, appetite and metabolism. Lack of it can therefore cause problems for the stressed executive.

Testosterone and cortisol are perhaps the most important distinguishing hormones between men and women in leadership roles. Men have ten times the testosterone as women that lead to competition, ambition and risk taking. Women are more affected by cortisol, known as the 'stress hormone'. It increases blood pressure and blood sugar and reduces immune responses and responses to stress. (Cortisol is a biological marker of the threat response. Feelings of low status provoke the kind of cortisol elevation associated with sleep deprivation and chronic anxiety.)

The SCARF model and Executive Gremlins

David Rock's SCARF article (first published in 2008) discussed the world of increasing interconnectedness and rapid change and the need for an improvement in the way people work together. He explores the theory relating to minimizing threat and maximizing reward (Gordon 2000). Simply put, when we meet people we perceive friend or foe.

John Herbert and John Coates, two Cambridge researchers, found that the amount of money a male financial trader makes in a day is correlated with his testosterone level and that a trader's level at the beginning of a day is strongly predictive of success that day, suggesting that stock market performance is positively affected by testosterone. However, they qualified their research by saying that whilst high levels may correlate with success it does so by reducing risk aversion. Whilst low risk aversion may be desirable in a 'bull market' (when stocks are rising) it is less desirable in a 'bear market'. They noted that other studies showed that prolonged elevation in testosterone levels leads to impulsivity, sensation seeking and harmful risk taking. We saw this contribute to the stock market collapse in 2008–9 (as a result of risk taking with subprime mortgages). It also contributes to market volatility and 'boom and bust' cycles. They suggested that men should reduce testosterone levels or simply hire more women. This lends weight to Harriet Harman's comment that 'if Lehman brothers had been run by Lehman sisters the bank would not have collapsed'. Along with many other people involved in the gender debate, I believe the optimal solution would be to have men and women running businesses.

SCARF

Dr David Rock's original article focused on five areas: Status, Certainty, Autonomy, Relatedness and Fairness.

S: *Status* is about relative importance to others.

C: *Certainty* is about being able to predict what will happen next.

A: *Autonomy* concerns a sense of feeling in control over events.

R: *Relatedness* is a sense of safety with others.

F: *Fairness* reflects a perception of fair exchanges between people.

Executives need to work differently in relation to threats and rewards. I have looked at The SCARF model and how this fits with The Executive Advantage 10-Step Solution for Resilient 21st-century Leaders©. The SCARF model was developed as an easy way to remember and act upon the social triggers that can generate both the 'approach' and 'avoid' responses. (The approach–avoid mechanism is the process whereby the brain labels a situation as either 'good' (and releases the 'happy drug' dopamine), or 'bad' and therefore generates a threat response.)

Executive advantage research focuses on deep-seated fears (Executive Gremlins) and how they manifest in the context of the organization. Tensions that manifest as anxiety move from being a problem for the individual to a strategic organizational problem that erodes profit and organizational success.

Status

The Executive Gremlins that manifest in relation to status are those labelled 'Unimportant' or 'Not good enough' in my model. The SCARF article referenced the work of Marmot, who said that 'status is the most significant determinant of human longevity and health', and Sapolski (2002) who found that 'in primate communities, status equals survival: higher status monkeys have lower baseline cortisol levels, live longer, and are healthier'. Basically, we are biologically programmed to care about status as it favours our survival. It is always comparative – having a new car at a party provides status until someone turns up with a bigger, more expensive one. The neural circuitry which processes status is similar to that which processes numbers and operates even when the stakes are meaningless. Understanding this need is important for leaders as they can learn to deal with situations that create a threat response, for example performance appraisals, or feedback. Things like 360-degree feedback reviews are therefore minefields. In numerous case studies, I observed that status is a core need for many people. The existential fear of being 'Unimportant' or a 'toothless old lion' emerges as people become fearful of loss of status as they get older.

Executives with the fear of being 'Unimportant' leading to loss of status often surround themselves with the trappings of success. It is the Executive Gremlin or 'little voice in the head' that sometimes leads to poor decision making. They will avoid situations that they fear will make them feel unimportant and approach those that make them feel important.

Certainty

In the SCARF model the brain is depicted as a being a pattern-recognition machine that is constantly trying to predict the near future. The brain craves certainty so that it can predict what will happen next. The brain draws on memories of what has happened in the past to predict and create expectations based on our experiences. The brain relies on long-established neural connections in the basal ganglia and motor cortex that have in effect hardwired the situation and the individual's response to it. This frees people to do more things at once as the 'basics' are covered (eg driving a car and talking). However, if the brain registers ambiguity or confusion it will bring up an error signal (eg the car in front brakes suddenly). The working memory is diminished and full attention must be given to the task in hand (driving). Uncertainty registers as a gap, a tension, something that must be corrected before we feel comfortable again. This is why people crave certainty. Mild uncertainty may be a good thing as it may be perceived as a challenge and creates a mild threat response that results in a release of adrenaline and dopamine – which spark curiosity and energize people. However, too much uncertainty will almost certainly result in loss of focus, and poor decision making, leading to poor performance. Leaders must seek out ways to give people certainty, to create teams and accurate maps of the organization that promote certainty.

This may be related to organizations as people like to be right. We all like to believe that what has happened before will probably determine what will happen in the future because that makes us feel safe. However, this is not always so. It is OK sometimes to be 'wrong and happy', ie seeing that someone else's solution is better than our own, or looking at a situation from a completely different angle.

We all have our own view of the world based on our own personal journey and life experiences from the past, which form our belief systems and create filters. These in turn influence how we perceive our present and future situations and possibilities. This can lead to us having a distorted view of a situation. We may enter into a situation and view it completely differently from another person because our perception of events is different due to our own personal beliefs and unique neural pathways and patterns.

This could be because uncertainty generates 'error' responses in the orbital frontal cortex (OFC) that take attention away from a task, forcing us to focus on the error (Hedden and Gabrieli 2006). If someone is not congruent in their communication this can fire up errors in the OFC. Similarly, creating certainty is pleasurable because mental maps are recalled. We believe we are 'right'. Meeting expectations generates an increase in dopamine levels in the brain, which creates a reward response (Schulz, 1999).

Autonomy

This area is all about control or the perception of control over our environment. As long as people feel they have control and choice over their world, stress remains manageable. That is why people will sacrifice money for the perception of freedom and why being micro managed may generate a strong threat response. Research has shown that the reason people decide to work for themselves is autonomy and work–life balance, yet most people who work for themselves work much longer hours – it is the perception that they have control that is important. The SCARF model describes how autonomy decreases when working in teams but is compensated for by an increase in status, certainty and relatedness.

CASE STUDY

Let's revisit the coaching client who went on maternity leave, and who found a locum to cover and agreed the scope of his role in detail. He wanted to do a good job. She kept in touch whilst she was away and after about three months discovered that he had changed the structure of her board report. She was incandescent with rage – a reaction far greater than the scale of the offence. This normally reasonable gifted woman could not believe his temerity. By using the Executive Advantage 10-Step Solution© she identified that she had fears of being Unimportant and Powerless. Once we established that she had not said he couldn't change it and that it was probably a well-intentioned act, she was able to see where she had overreacted to the situation and she was able to choose different behaviours and make better decisions. Under the SCARF model we can see that her response related to her need for Autonomy. By changing her report he threatened it and she perceived a foe and responded accordingly.

Relatedness

The SCARF model defines this as whether an individual is 'in' or 'out' of a social group. It describes the formation of 'tribes' and belonging. Healthy relationships require trust and empathy but the brain's ability to feel these is shaped by whether they are perceived as part of the same social group. This is why teams tend to dislike opposing teams or in siloed organizations why one part of the business dislikes and is antagonistic towards another. This is why care must be taken when putting together diverse teams. Whilst diversity is perceived as a good thing to avoid 'group think', it is more difficult to put difference together without triggering a threat response. Trust cannot be assumed as the brain views difference as a threat. Once people make a strong social connection their brains will secrete oxytocin (linked to affection, maternal affection and sexual arousal), which disarms the threat response. Thus leaders who strive for inclusion and minimize situations in which people feel rejected create an environment that supports maximum performance. This is particularly hard to do when companies are going through change or downsizing. Relatedness needs relate to the patterns and beliefs around feeling the fear of being Unlovable or disliked under the executive advantage model. The decision that someone is friend or foe happens quickly and impacts brain functioning (Carter and Pelphrey 2008). When people are perceived as competitors the capacity to empathize drops significantly (Singer *et al* 2006).

CASE STUDY

In an earlier example, I described a CEO who made some poor decisions that impacted on a director's ability to deliver a major IT transformational programme. We saw how the new CEO decided to humiliate the director at the sales conference in public. The director was seriously embarrassed and angry. By using the Executive Advantage 10-Step Solution© we identified that his 'Unlovable' process had been activated. He felt all respect had been stripped away in front of his peers and his staff. The new CEO had a strong ego and needed to appear Important and had therefore chosen to move the blame onto the director. In protecting his own fear, he had 'pressed' on his director's. In neuroscience terms, my client's need for Relatedness was undermined and his brain perceived a threat response. His prefrontal cortex shut down and adrenaline was released into his bloodstream. His body reacted to the threat by shaking and he felt sick.

Fairness

In the SCARF model fairness is described as 'fair exchanges that are intrinsically rewarding', whilst 'unfair exchanges generate a strong threat response' (Tabibnia and Lieberman 2007). This is relevant to this book because it involves dealing with a threat response and building resilience. If a person has a perception that an event has been unfair then their brain will generate a strong threat response in the limbic system, stirring hostility and lack of trust. It is similar to status in that fairness tends to be relative.

People are more satisfied with a minimal reward via a fair exchange than an unfair exchange that generates more reward. Apparently, the reward response in the brain to an experience that is fair is similar to that produced by eating chocolate! Fairness is why people fight and die for causes. Thus leaders must attempt to be fair at all times even if the news is not great. Having favourites will generate a threat response in others. For example 'felt-fair pay' is an important element in bonus calculations – people are happy to earn a smaller bonus as long as it isn't smaller than anyone else's. Fairness shows up in executive advantage when someone feels that a leader has not been fair. Why will vary from individual to individual. For example, someone with a need to feel important, lovable or good enough will find their Executive Gremlins activated if they are left out of an important meeting, or given extra work, because it isn't perceived as 'fair'. The tendency to *react* rather than *respond* will come into play. The brain recognizes patterns from the past where experiences were not fair and a knee-jerk automatic reaction occurs.

CASE STUDY

A coaching client reported that he had been made sales director after being involved as technical director for many years, since the start up of the business. The company sold large IT projects into pharmaceutical companies with very long sales cycles. They were doing better than the industry average so my client perceived it was unfair that he was being berated for not hitting quarterly targets. However, we were able to identify that he had a 'Not good enough' fear, based on events that had happened to him in the past (he had been a child prodigy/genius chess player at the age of five and had never been allowed to play, as he had been given a 'gift'). His connection to that particular memory was very strong and quite upsetting. Despite his perception of the current situation as unfair, he was able to make new decisions in his dealings with the MD once he knew what was driving his own behaviour. He was therefore able to create new insights and new neural pathways that led to better decision making. He was able to refocus, became more confident and hit target.

Fairness is served by transparency and consistency. Leaders should share information to keep people engaged and motivated. Even in cutback situations, employees will see it as fair if a consistent approach is taken and there is a clear rationale for the choices made.

Twenty-first-century leaders in organizations will need to make sure they provide certainty and as much information as they can. People also need to feel they have autonomy and some control over their own destiny. Astute leaders minimize the threat response by giving people permission to exercise control when it's possible to do so. People won't support initiatives that are imposed upon them, so the more they are involved in the planning process, the smoother things will go. If you understand your own Executive Gremlins, and if you are self-aware, you will be more effective. A self-aware leader modifies their own behaviour in the moment to alleviate organizational stress. They are flexible and create agile organizations. Motivation and creativity flourish. Being spontaneous is a vital tool to being an authentic, resilient 21st-century leader. If leaders can also apply the SCARF model, to increase creativity and reduce threats, we will have better, more prosperous organizations.

Neuroleadership and gender – are we wired differently?

There has seldom been a greater divide between what intelligent, enlightened opinion presumes – that men and women have the same brain – and what science knows – that they do not.

Dr Anne Moir, neuropsychologist

She claims the 'irrefutable scientific truth' that the differences between men and women are not just physical but also neurological. The differences in our brain wiring cause us to think, feel and behave differently. She believes that is why men and women respond differently to emotional and situational 'triggers' and that neurochemistry affects things like confidence and competition. Her research indicates that women lack confidence and do not step up in the same way as men do because of the effect of, or rather lack of, testosterone.

When I was writing this book, I was thinking creatively for long periods. Towards the deadline for finishing my manuscript, as I was integrating the leaders' views into my text, I began to feel overloaded and started making silly mistakes in my real life. I forgot to book my flights to a business conference ahead and had to pay almost double. I annoyed my partner by firing off knee-jerk texts to him in a panic that involved checking he was doing things. I never find detail easy and this stage was hard work for my brain. I finally had an insight – my prefrontal cortex was overloaded and my emotions were running riot because I felt Out of control and Not good enough. By understanding what was going on and labelling it, my limbic system calmed down, I was able to refocus and make decisions.

The brain also has a sex, just like the body (Moir and Jessel 1992). The male foetus in the womb produces male hormones, including testosterone, triggered by the Y chromosome. The resulting cascade of male genes is what causes male characteristics and behaviours later in life. Without these the foetus would remain female with female behaviours and characteristics. Children's development is affected by testosterone and there is a negative correlation between high levels of testosterone and low language and social skills. This fits with the classic pattern of sex differences found in learning and behaviour. For example, girls do better in language and communication subjects than boys. In adulthood, women are better verbally equipped. A Yale University study showed via scanning that whereas men use the left side of the brain to process verbal information, women use both sides. Subsequent studies have shown that in general the cerebral cortex is more bilaterally organized in women than in men, showing that women use both sides of their brain. While it is contested by neuroscientists that anyone can multi-task, it may be why women are regarded as being able to – their brains are networked and interconnected, whereas men compartmentalize. This can work for and against women. Women tend to see consequences and the whole picture but have difficulty switching off, so we take work problems home, and worry about home and children whilst we are at work. Men are more able to separate the two. In leader interviews, I repeatedly heard from men that they are more able to compartmentalize and therefore suffer less in this respect.

Women have larger prefrontal cortex areas and they mature faster – which means she has better brakes on the reactive, primitive area of the brain than the male. This is sometimes why he has more difficulty controlling his anger and impulsive behaviour. The amygdala generates emotional feeling and is the emotional memory processor. It is larger in the male and less under the control of the prefrontal cortex than in the female. Men process memories globally in the right amygdala, women in complex detail in the left. She will remember more detail generally as the hippocampus is larger and more active in women. The result of this is she remembers more negatives, her filters get stronger and is one reason why more women suffer from depression – women report feeling greater pain. Whether this is real or perceptual, it seems likely they are actually 'feeling' it (as the brain doesn't know the difference between reality and suggestion) and that there is a case for a process to help identify what is driving their anxiety. Case study research into executive anxiety illustrated that whilst both men and women experience it, and value working on it in the safety of a coaching relationship, women seem happier to bring it up earlier in the coaching relationship and admit to 'weakness' more readily.

The female brain is more active than the male. Blood flows faster through the female brain, giving her the oxygen and glucose necessary to fuel faster processing. Eventually our brains shrink and change with age. Men lose more brain tissue, especially in the left frontal cortex, the part of the brain that thinks about consequences and provides self-control. Which is perhaps why men are said to have mid-life crises!

Men have more impulses but they lose the ability to consider long-term consequences.

Ruben Gur, neurologist

Does SCARF apply differently to men and women?

Yes and no. Yes, because women are likely to be affected to a greater or lesser extent by different elements because of the effects of hormones, and no because many elements apply equally to both genders.

Status

It is unclear whether the SCARF research was based on just males or males and females. Much research is based on males as females have monthly hormone fluctuations that can skew results. It seems possible that it was undertaken on men (who are also affected by hormones but not in monthly cycles), who have 10–20 times more testosterone than women, leading to more aggressive, competitive behaviour and need for status. It may be an area that is a more common need for men, though I know plenty of women who need status too! However, it is also more consistent with my research and leader interviews – men mentioned the effect of becoming more mature with age (as testosterone levels drop) and women mentioned not being as confident or competitive as younger men.

Women often fear being overlooked, of not being good enough for board positions, even not looking as good, which undermines their confidence. They consistently underestimate their abilities, allowing men to gain promotion to executive boards when they are just as capable.

Similarly, women with 'Not good enough' fears will keep working harder and harder to prove that they *are* good enough. Organizations often do well from them, but the women themselves often forget to self-promote in the process. Women lack confidence partly because of negative beliefs they hold about themselves. In order to get more women on boards they need to achieve a real improvement in confidence. The Not good enough fear also shows up in women trying to be superwomen. (We explore more about women and 21st-century leadership in Chapter 6.)

Certainty

This is often a high need area for women as they are more risk averse than men. Cortisol is released in stressful situations. High levels of cortisol stay elevated for longer in women and can create anxiety in highly political business environments. However, this is largely because organizations have a preponderance of men. The influence of more women in the workplace, especially at senior levels, would promote a positive culture shift.

Autonomy

When women's brains are developing in the womb they are not flooded by testosterone like men's and as a consequence they grow up with better language skills and higher levels of social and emotional needs. They seek out relationships and harmony. Their need for autonomy is often linked to wanting to be able to get everything done. Women report flexibility as being a core driver in whether to stay in a job or leave, whether to seek promotion, and they will put up with a lot to gain it. For instance, very few women with flexible work arrangements will look for another job as they perceive they would have less flexibility. Similarly, women considering having a baby will often self-select out of a promotion opportunity 'just in case'. This is often driven by a desire to control their environment as they perceive that it is better to work within the environment they know than to risk trying to navigate a new one.

Relatedness

Relatedness is particularly important to most women. We are all familiar with the 'fight or flight' response to stress. Shelley Taylor put forward a different point of view in her book *The Tending Instinct* when she realized that the traditional theory was based on research conducted on male rats and humans. She claims that women are hardwired to cope with stress differently. Instead of fighting or fleeing, which would be adaptive for a hunter being chased by a predator, women's instincts lead them to protect their offspring (tending) and to look to others for support (befriending). She contends that if we do not receive tending, or have social support, we are at heightened risk of stress-related illness.

Fairness

In their article 'The pains and pleasures of social life' Eisenberger and Lieberman describe a woman who felt she was given more than her 'fair share' of work by her partner. They describe how the brain experiences social/emotional pain in the same way as it experiences physical pain. Therefore it was unclear whether the woman was experiencing upset because she was given more work or because it was insulting (because she is a woman) and therefore intrinsically unfair.

All individuals experience fear, though there are considerable differences in how we respond to stress and pain and how willing we are to discuss and deal with them. Research for the Executive Advantage 10-Step Solution© showed that most coaching clients felt the most valuable part of the coaching was the help given to get through the stress surrounding a particularly difficult situation, having a safe place to share. Having 'labelled' these fears or patterns it appeared that more women suffered with 'Unlovable' and 'Guilty', whilst more men suffered with feeling 'Powerless' and 'Unimportant'. There were equal numbers feeling 'Not good enough'. Whilst both sexes may experience different fears in larger numbers, when they are affected by the same fear they seemed to be affected in similar ways. There is a slight tendency for women to cry when angry and for men to express anger in a more overt way. What is clear is that the identification of a fear and the labelling process calm the limbic system and reduce the emotional response, which in turn allows an individual's prefrontal cortex to wake up, to think more clearly, and to make new choices in stressful situations.

Both The Executive Advantage 10-Step Solution described in Chapter 4 and neuroleadership are solutions that benefit from deeper study than this book allows. Mind training can be very helpful for some people.

The benefits of mind training and the 10-Step Solution:

- calming the mind;
- learning to listen to your thoughts and becoming aware of unhelpful attitudes;
- making better decisions;
- improving attention;
- understanding emotions and how they derail business plans;
- clarifying intentions;
- improving problem solving;
- becoming more disciplined;
- improving acceptance and patience;
- engaging in deep listening.

Other suggestions that have worked for me and for some of the leaders interviewed include:

- exercise;
- breathing exercises;
- self-awareness training;
- nutrition and health;
- psychotherapy;
- counselling;
- executive coaching.

Actions

- Explore neuroscience via workshops, seminars and reading.
- Follow the work of David Rock and The Neuroleadership Group.
- Get a suitably qualified coach (**www.transition-coaching.co.uk**).
- Consider mind training.

In the next chapter we will explore how the Executive Advantage 10-Step Solution for 21st-century Leaders© can help women leaders to become more successful and help organizations to become more inclusive and have more women on boards.

Women on the edge

In the last chapter I explained neuroleadership, including how the male and female brains are different and how this affects our relationship with stress, fear and Executive Gremlins. This chapter is called 'Women on the edge' for two reasons: first, because women are finally on the edge of achieving greater success in greater numbers than ever before, and second, because Executive Gremlins in women adversely affect their confidence and so they may be on the edge mentally. It is concerned with the real executive advantage (for both men and women) to be obtained by understanding and overcoming the self-limiting beliefs that hold women back.

Are women more affected by executive anxiety and Executive Gremlins than men? Probably not. Are they more willing than men to talk about them and admit weakness? Probably.

> *Men have heart attacks, women talk about it, they are wired differently in the brain – men don't share pain.*
>
> **Board director, FTSE 500 IT company**

In my research for this book I asked the following questions:

Are women more affected by stress than men?

> *No, lots of men are big girls' blouses!*
>
> **Chairman**

> *Men have heart attacks, women talk about it.*
>
> **Male MD**

I do not think that women are more affected by stress than men but do believe that women tend to talk about it more and are more willing to let it show. Thought leaders from the world of neuro-leadership largely concur. Whilst male and female brains are physio-logically similar, men and women use them differently and are affected differently by chemicals and hormones. Women's brains *are* 'wired differently' from men's.

I have worked with numerous women in top jobs in the City and they love working on their Executive Gremlins. They relate easily to the concept and are not afraid to open up to the process of look-ing at them. Whilst men find it equally helpful, it takes longer to get to it in most coaching interventions. We have to spend longer looking at the organizational issues before we get down to exploring Executive Gremlins.

> *Women have higher-level emotional skills and better impulse control but basically react the same.*
>
> **Male CEO**

> *My wife enabled me to succeed because she took care of everything else; stress is more debilitating for men because they don't share.*
>
> **Male CEO**

> *Women internalize and blame themselves for problems whereas men externalize and blame others – women don't compartmentalize as well as men; if either home or work derails it affects the other.*
>
> **Group HR director**

Do you believe there is discrimination against women at any level?

The vast majority of respondents said that there was no overt discrimination now but a lot of discrimination comes from unconscious bias. Having said that, I came across a number of women who had been subjected to horrendous treatment, including things that would be labelled as discriminatory in law.

I interviewed an executive coach who had left corporate life due to an intense bullying situation. Having been happily employed for 15 years as a senior account manager in IT, she was assigned to work for a man who she believes wanted to get her out. He systematically undermined everything she did and she described being 'constantly in fear' and had a breakdown. He even called her into 'a meeting with HR' whilst she was on long-term sick leave and when she arrived there was no HR representative there.

> There was no HR rep there – he just shouted at me and I broke down and cried. He carried on and I just couldn't stop crying. On the way home I nearly hit a lorry because I was crying so hard. I had loved the company and been successful for 15 years and because of one boss I had to leave – I feel damaged forever.

She told me that she still retains traumatic feelings from that period despite counselling and psychotherapy. She feels vulnerable around 'certain types of men' although she is now '95 per cent' herself again.

Interviewing this woman and working with others who described similar experiences enabled me to deconstruct their experience using the 10-Step Solution. We identified Unimportant and Unlovable and Not good enough gremlins.

> There are still board members who think that 'women don't really cut it' but sometimes women become inflexible and defensive. Their passive–aggressive responses add to the downward spiral.

Female global director

Returning to 'the pendulum' mentioned in Chapter 3 regarding conflict, the passive–aggressive swing described reflects emotional leakage – the women were unable to control themselves. This is because, in the moment, the Executive Gremlin takes over, the prefrontal cortex has shut down, and the amygdala is registering a threat. We attack as a means of defence. When we experience a 'button push' we have a knee-jerk reaction and become aggressive.

> It [discrimination] is subtle, underground, not in your face. We must all be vigilant.
>
> **Female board director**

As Western women today, we are relatively lucky – we do have choice. In the Victorian era our career choices were extremely limited. Now the glass ceiling is, on the whole, perceptual rather than real in that men are not sitting at the top of organizations holding the door closed against us; they no longer seek to hold women back or perceive women to be less capable. They are not actively discriminating against us. Where discrimination exists it is largely unconscious bias, the result of someone 'not being like us' rather than a conscious discriminatory point of view (which tends to exist only in individuals I refer to as 'dinosaurs'). But we still have a problem.

> Women are still not making it to the top of any profession anywhere in the world.
>
> **Sheryl Sandberg, COO of Facebook**

The numbers tell the story clearly. Of 190 heads of state in the world only nine are women. Only 13 per cent of the world's parliamentarians are women. In UK corporations C-level (high-ranking) jobs top out at 15–16 per cent if we are lucky. In UK City institutions the numbers are as low as 3 per cent at MD level. Even in not-for-profit organizations where we tend to think there are more women, there are still only 20 per cent at the top. The Davies Report (2011) caused a stir but did it tell us anything new – did it just gain attention because the government and (perhaps even more worrying) because *men* had joined the debate? The report proposed that

FTSE 500 boards should aim for a minimum of 25 per cent female representation by 2015.

One year on from the Davies Report and the largest-ever increase in the percentage of women on boards has been seen. This reflects a growing recognition of the benefits to business, the economy and society by appointing more women to decision-making roles. The Cranfield School of Management female FTSE 500 report highlights that if the current momentum is maintained a record 26.7 per cent female board representation could be achieved by 2015. Businesses are now taking the issue seriously.

However, women still face harder choices between professional success and personal fulfilment. In a recent US study, two-thirds of top men had children, whilst only one-third of women at the top had. Why do women feel they have to sacrifice personal fulfilment in order to achieve success in business?

Why do some women drop out? People talk about the fixes – the things organizations need to do: the events, the mentoring, and the development programmes. I am one of these people – they are important, but there are also some fundamental things women need to do if we want to keep them in the workforce and change these awful statistics.

Women will never make it to the boardroom in significant numbers whilst they allow men to self-promote at their expense, continue to take on the lion's share of the work at home and turn down opportunities because of worrying about what they might lead to in the future. Women allow these things because they are controlled by their Executive Gremlins.

Women need to start believing in themselves and self-promote

When I was at (a girls') school I noticed that all the girls would study for exams and go to all the lessons, whilst the boys at their schools bunked off lessons and revised at the very last minute. I had an older, charismatic, tennis-playing brother. Whilst I was certainly no swot I would come home after exams convinced that I had failed and then later be delighted to learn that I had passed. My brother would come home believing he was top of the class – until he got his results! I was considered to be a rebel at school because I questioned and didn't always study as hard as others but that was nothing compared to my brother. The truth is he had absolute self-belief in his abilities whilst I constantly questioned myself. I noticed that most of the girls did. We questioned the way we looked, who was the most popular, how clever we were (reflecting fears of being Unlovable, Stupid and Unimportant).

Fast forward a few years and nothing much has changed. Research shows that women systematically underestimate their abilities. When men go for promotion with 80 per cent of the skills required they bang the table and say they are perfect for the job and start talking about pay. A woman with the same set of skills will focus on the 20 per cent she doesn't have and start explaining how hard she will work to overcome her failings. Only 7 per cent of women entering the workplace ever mention starting pay whilst the majority of young men negotiate. (This reflects fears of being Unimportant, Stupid and Not Good Enough.)

CASE STUDY

There is a hugely successful TV programme in the UK called *The Apprentice*. In the final episode of the 2011 programme the front runner, who had won 10 out of 11 tasks over the weeks, was asked how she did it. She looked embarrassed and said she was just lucky and had worked hard. The interviewer's face said it all. She came second. There may have been other reasons but it is typical of what women do when given the opportunity to self-promote.

Ask a successful woman why she has made it and she will tell you about luck, other people, circumstances, hard work. Ask a guy and he may well say 'I'm great!' or words to that effect. Who do you think the employer will choose? By the time we get to decisions about board appointments women's names are not even on the list – chairmen are not deliberately anti-women, women are just not on their radar in large enough numbers. Most company board directors are not prejudiced and there is greater diversity of thinking at the top. However, many women *perceive* that it is still there and in truth it does seem to vary by industry.

Do women 'stand up and be counted'?

Definitely not – it's their number one issue. Women dislike self-promotion and it has a huge impact on confidence. Women still have to work in a male organizational model.

Rachel Brushfield, career coach and researcher

Less so than men. It's the testosterone effect. Ninety-eight per cent of crimes and accidents are committed or caused by men. This is the same thing.

Group IT director, global business

The responses to this were mixed depending on the industries involved. The majority felt that they didn't. However, investment bankers, top tier consultants and IT new business sales directors are not perceived to have this problem. Even so, I have coached seemingly powerful and successful investment bankers and IT directors who do self-doubt behind the scenes. I have worked on Executive Gremlins with most of them at some point. Almost all agreed that 'most women' had this problem even if they didn't recognize it in themselves.

I didn't have a problem, no, but I have seen other women hold themselves back.

Female MD, global IT company

> *No, the ones that do are pretend men. I heard executive women referred to as 'blokes with boobs' or 'women with codpieces'!*

MD, global IT company

> *There are some women who try to be men. They are more aggressive, particularly in big organizations like investment banking and hedge funds. Women communicate more about everything. They talk about the issues but they don't always self-promote. Men talk about business and self-promote but rarely talk about 'personal stuff'.*

CEO

Women need to stop being nice (need to be liked) and pouring the coffee in important meetings whilst men climb over them to get to the top. When we get the chance to be successful do we fear it because it sits so uncomfortably with our own self-perception? Women who make it need to encourage others to follow – whatever it takes, putting their names up for promotion, mentoring younger women. They must not pull up the ladder. I have found in my career that it is not always the people you expect who either help you or pull up the ladder.

Don't try to be superwomen!

Women still do twice as much housework and take on three times as much of the childcare responsibilities as men. So they are doing two or three jobs whilst men are doing one. Of course they have more time for networking and self-promotion!

CASE STUDY

I worked with an investment bank, coaching their senior executive women through maternity. We met once during the three months before they went on maternity leave, once before they came back, and once again when they had been back at work between one and three months. Sometimes these executive women decided to continue after their maternity. This is an area where women need a lot of support as they are juggling momentous personal issues with sometimes conflicting work issues. Some are extremely well organized and have their role completely delegated and planned, but have not thought much about plans for the baby, others are totally swept up in their pregnancies and haven't thought that much about work. Whichever it is, they all seem to present with executive fears: 'Will they keep my job open for me?' 'Will they change things whilst I'm away?' 'My boss will be mean to me when I go back.' 'What if I can't cope with everything?' 'How will I feel about leaving my baby for a transatlantic trip?' 'Supposing the baby gets more attached to the nanny than to me.'

By supporting them through their pregnancies and offering them support back into these senior executive roles, the bank has realized that they are more likely to retain them at a time when men are still perceiving 'the best' to mean like them and there is still a serious shortage of senior women at the top.

Men who stay at home are still perceived as rather odd or lacking in something but it is one of the hardest jobs in the world and making the decision to do that is difficult whether you are a man or a woman. Men who stay at home have reported that they feel undermined, 'Not good enough' and 'Powerless' – women who stay at home report the same. They require a strong sense of self-worth to avoid resentment.

However, studies have shown that equal partnerships at home have lower divorce rates and better sex lives, though how this was measured I am not quite sure!

I have three stepsons from a previous relationship whom I support and adore, several godchildren, a much younger boyfriend, two gorgeous golden retrievers, two aged parents and no other relatives to help, plus an active social life. I couldn't manage all of these and have a successful career without help. I have an executive assistant for work, a Girl Friday, a cleaner, a personal trainer, a handyman, a pool man and a gardener. Most of the 'inspirational women' I know either have house husbands or help. Don't try to be superwomen!

Use your gender difference; don't just be a stereotype

Women are wired differently from men. We have different brains and neurochemistry and are very affected by hormones. As I explained in Chapter 5, men's systems are flooded with testosterone from an early age, which drives them to compete and win. Women are more affected by stress-inducing cortisol partly because their levels take longer to come down. They have higher relational needs, which show up in Executive Gremlins of 'Unlovable' or 'Not good enough'.

Women will stop going for promotions if they are even thinking about having a baby or taking some time out. Men tend to keep their plans to themselves until they need to share them and are constantly seeking promotion.

> When I was running an executive women's programme with the investment bank's equities division I was constantly being asked about how to make it to MD (not even C-suite level) and, once they trusted me, when the best time was to have a baby. It was no surprise when the credit crunch hit in banking that a huge number of women of childbearing age decided to 'off ramp'.

Some of the women who were asking about planning to have babies didn't even have boyfriends or husbands! Women need to stay in the game until the day they want to get out. They must keep their choices open. They should be loyal but not to the degree that they limit their choices.

The double glass ceiling

My bosses are men. That is how it is. Men gave me a PhD and pay my salary. Men promote me and men will fire me one day.

Adam, private sector (extracted from Stonewall report

'The double-glazed glass ceiling')

As a woman you've already got one strike against you in terms of a diversity box that you check. As a lesbian that's the second one as well. If you're an ethnic minority lesbian you've got three.

Georgia, private sector (Stonewall report)

In the process of writing this book, I realized that I did not understand whether gay women acted in the same way as straight women when it comes to issues of promotion and confidence. I spoke to two very senior women who were 'out' (public and private sectors) and two who were not. The results were consistent. They directed me to a very helpful article produced by Stonewall which made the point that:

Gay women have to put their hands up twice, once as a woman and again as being gay.

The interviewees concurred with this article. They also made the point that it was considerably easier to be confident when they were 'out' since they didn't have to live an inauthentic existence where people assumed they had no social life. They had decided they'd rather admit that they were gay and face possible prejudice for it. One said that 'coming out' to self and then to family was actually a process of personal growth that straight people do not have to face. Two of the women had faced open discrimination at work. Men had made comments to other people about their sexuality. Another woman was asked bluntly by her boss if she was gay. Whilst this may seem a step too far to some, she actually decided to tell him that she was gay and to come out at work. She describes this as empowering. He was asking from a 'good place' – he commented that it was obvious she was in a stable, loving relationship and that was considered very important to senior executives in business. She found this immensely helpful in boosting her confidence as she was able to be more authentic. This woman is probably the most senior 'out' role model in the City. She regularly presents at conferences and dinners and supports women in her own organization via mentoring. When I asked her about this, she said that when she came up through the ranks there were fewer role models. Working with Executive Gremlins is always personally challenging, but having role models helps. Finding successful gay women to speak out about their experience is extremely helpful to women seeking career progression. Most described feeling disregarded and worried about how others would react to them (reflecting an Unlovable fear). Some took on a more masculine persona. It is very difficult to be authentic whilst hiding your true self. The executive advantage solution will help you to identify what is holding you back.

> I am more comfortable about being a role model now that I know I am not on a pedestal. Making a difference is a huge responsibility but a great opportunity.
>
> **Managing partner, City firm**

When I discussed discrimination with this managing partner she felt that it was largely unconscious. She gave the example of a woman who was suitable for promotion and who was pregnant. She promoted her anyway. This raises the question: 'How many men would have done this?' One woman talked about when she was sent to Afghanistan:

> There were about 2,000 people in the mess tents of all ranks but very few women – when I walked in it was like the place stood still – a 'tumbleweed' moment!

She went on to describe herself in that moment as:

> More of a GI Jemima than a GI Jane – I was not looking glamorous!

Whilst this would probably have been difficult for any woman, being gay made this especially hard. A straight colleague of hers described being on a tour of duty on a ship and mentioned that she 'gave off an aura' to avoid unwanted attention.

Overall, there does not appear to be any difference regarding confidence and stepping up between gay or straight women. They are just as affected by family issues and work–life balance as their straight colleagues.

Why aren't there more women on boards?

Why aren't there enough women on boards? The answer is simple: historically they haven't been encouraged to get there by organizations; and second, women 'get in their own way'.

The publication in the UK of the Davies Report focused minds. There are many thought leaders writing about the subject. Alison Maitland and Avivah Wittenberg-Cox (authors of *Why Women Mean Business*, 2008) wrote compellingly about the economic realities of ignoring the gender problem. Business schools have provided great research on the subject yet ironically their female student intakes still only make up 30 per cent of the total – substantially less than legal and medical schools. This could exacerbate the problem of parity in the future senior leadership of corporations. Cranfield's notable report 'A decade of delay', published in 2008, portrayed a depressing view of women on boards. Forward-thinking organizations have been writing about the problem for years, yet little has changed. McKinsey reports have suggested that companies with the greatest gender diversity in top management outperformed their sector average in terms of return on equity, though there is counter evidence to suggest that this is not the case. A recent Evershed's report confirmed that organizations with more diverse boards, with more women on them, were more profitable. Inclusive leadership is a fundamentally necessary capability for 21st-century leaders. Appointing more women to boards is a fundamental element of inclusion.

CASE STUDY

When I joined the investment bank as an FVP, I was able to conduct ethnographic research and 'go native' as a senior woman in a top tier organization. We ran a number of unique and compelling programmes for women but these were still paid lip service to by people at all levels in the organization. Women were still not always taken seriously and were given a hard time when they returned to work after maternity leave or when seeking promotion. We were typical of the top five.

Yet these same organizations sought recognition as female-friendly places and won awards for their innovative approaches. At graduate intake, investment banks take on average 51 per cent female graduates, yet these numbers dwindle to 28 per cent when they reach VP/director level and only 3 per cent in some client-facing roles by the time they would be expecting to be promoted to FVP/MD. Young women would come in believing there was no problem and were often dismissive of women's programmes, yet they often disclosed to me that they didn't know when they were going to be able to have children or didn't see the point of having them if they never saw their children due to workload if they wanted to 'make it'. Or they weren't sure they wanted the fairly linear progression offered. Others doubted their own abilities and focused on what they didn't have rather than their talent. Yet there were women who made it, the rare role model that seemed to have it all. They were powerful, significant women who believed in themselves and had the confidence to push through and succeed. So why was this so difficult for the rest? Additionally, why were there not more women on boards generally – was it only about having children? My research for this book suggests not.

Historically, women have been discriminated against in the workplace. There were plenty of factory floors where the norm was unequal pay (See the movie *Made in Dagenham*) and a dearth of women were found at the top table. Board members in the Western world largely fitted the stereotype of white, middle-aged and middle-class male and largely recruited to their own image. Business was done over golf or drinks after work and it was pretty much accepted that this was the norm. We have all heard of the old boy clubs. However, times have changed and women are not generally discriminated against (apart from isolated incidents). There is still a pay gap, although this is being closed over time. The fact that women accept work at lower pay in today's world is interesting. I have worked with women who know that they are paid less yet don't confront it. They fear losing their jobs or their next promotion if they assert themselves. This is a confidence issue driven by Executive Gremlins (though the organizations with inequitable pay are also responsible). In working with many boards, CEOs repeatedly report that they cannot find good women to promote or hire. Or they hire them as a last-ditch effort to save an underperforming business in order to effect a high-risk turnaround. Unsurprisingly, some of these women fail. Dr Michelle Ryan and Professor Alex Haslam's research into 'The glass cliff' (University of Exeter 2005) challenges the emerging idea that women on company boards are responsible for corporate decline, revealing that the positions women attain are often more precarious than those offered to similarly qualified men!

Does lack of confidence play a part in women not making it onto boards?

Yes, but the more you do it the more confident you become.

Female director, plc

This question provoked a resounding 'Yes' as the number one issue for women to address and the reason why more women do not make it onto boards. The Executive Advantage 10-Step Solution for Resilient 21st-century Leaders© is the powerful tool for improving confidence. Women who can understand their Executive Gremlins and work out helpful strategies for overcoming them will have an executive advantage.

Men get more credit because they claim it. Women ask 'Am I good enough?'
They tend to focus on getting the job done.

Operations director, plc

Yes, but Gen Y women are more confident so things may change.

Female HR director

A number of people raised the issue of 'Gen Y'. They mentioned that both sexes have concerns now about when to have children and the fact that both parents often have to work in order to own their own properties. Also, young men want sabbaticals and more flexibility as much as do women. Time will tell as 'Gen Y-ers' reach the boardroom. Hopefully, the outcome will be positive as young men with more open ideas reach the top and women step up in greater numbers.

Do women go after promotion as aggressively as men?

This question elicited a very strong 'No' response. A number of leaders quoted the '80/20 rule' The 80/20 applies to where a man with 80 per cent of the skills for a promotion will go for the job and position themselves as perfect for the role. A woman with 80 per cent will go to the interview but explain the 20 per cent she doesn't have and how she will work hard to overcome her short-comings. This leads to a lack of confidence – the woman's and the person hiring.

> *Very capable women self-doubt.*
>
> **Male COO, financial services**

> *No, women are more intuitive and likely to support others. They hope to be noticed but feel really uncomfortable about pushing.*
>
> **Male CEO**

> *Women who do are regarded as 'power bitches', men as successful and ambitious.*
>
> **Female HR board director**

> *Women should leave sometimes and they don't jump. They are too loyal, partly for the childcare reasons.*
>
> **Headhunter**

> *No, women have more compromises. They are hugely conflicted because they are dedicated to home. Men compartmentalize better.*
>
> **Male CEO**

Have you promoted women onto boards and what special considerations did you have?

Very few had, although they had often recommended, probably reflecting the shortage of women in chair or CEO roles. Very few had any special considerations other than being aware of unconscious bias. Several women admitted that they were guilty of only recommending men themselves, including the head of a women's network before she realized that she was adding to the problem and publicly offered to change in the future!

> *50–60 per cent of my teams are always female. Women sales executives are better. They listen and deliver what the customer asks for. Men don't listen as well and expand requests to include other things.*
>
> **Male MD, global IT**

> *I have promoted women and don't have special considerations. I believe in the best person for the job but am conscious there is still the 'old bugger generation' which sometimes inhibits. Pipeline becomes difficult if women are 'token'. The Davies Report has made it difficult to fire underperforming female executives. An MD in one company created two jobs for women to meet targets – I didn't know what they did.*
>
> **COO, financial services organization**

> *I look at skill sets. I proactively pick women if I can. Unconscious bias exists in all of us. Board-level appointments will be affected as most members don't understand the filters through which they perceive the world.*
>
> **Female global director**

> *When I was appointed I was benchmarked internally and externally but I still heard comments about me getting the job because I was a woman.*
>
> **Female board director**

Why do chairs and CEOs find it difficult to find good women and when they do, why do they always seem to turn up in HR, marketing and occasionally finance? Whilst these are critical roles, where are the female MDs, the sales directors and the commercial directors? They do exist but there is a distinct shortage. Are headhunters doing their jobs properly and are CEOs putting pressure on them to come up with more women? My research for this book suggested that people recruiting to boards should actively promote women and take risks. There is a tendency for the same names to be put forward for multiple non-executive roles. This does not solve the problem. Headhunters do 'heat seek' and there is a natural tendency for them to go to their existing networks first, which of course tend to be male, but there are many who are now recognizing and acting upon the problem. Similarly, if headhunters are asked for a 50 per cent female shortlist they will have to provide them.

As well as governments having a duty to encourage organizations to change and to hire and promote more women onto boards, and for organizations to take steps in the recruitment, development and promotion of women, women themselves must step up. They must focus on an immediate and visible improvement in their confidence, networking skills and activities. The gremlin of 'Not good enough' must be dealt with. They must learn to focus on their strengths and sell themselves.

Another key 21st-century leadership capability is 'authentic flexibility and agility'. However, in practice, when female executives are looking for flexibility as well as promotion they will often start with the former, which leads to questions about their commitment. Almost all the senior women I know who work flexibly started out doing a full-time role and then transitioned into a more flexible work pattern because the company could not afford to lose them. They did not find jobs on boards with flexibility already built in (other than non-executive roles, by which time they usually don't have problems with confidence and Executive Gremlins!). Neither do men. There is a significant shift in many people's perception regarding flexibility, with more and more people seeking to work in different ways (men as well as women). Organizations must engage with this if they are to attract the best talent (and ultimately to embrace other diverse groups in greater numbers, reflecting societal changes across the globe). Women need to learn to create their own opportunities and then to sell the benefits into their organizations. Being flexible and agile whilst retaining your authenticity is a key 21st-century leadership capability, but organizations need to learn to trust and value flexibility as well if they are to compete in global markets.

The women I know who have made it have sacrificed marriages, children and even health. So have some men. It is a hard road that not everyone wants to take. Women who want it badly enough can make it onto boards. Organizations need to help them to get there by creating inclusive working environments and targeting leaders on diversity. (See Chapter 8, 'The Executive Advantage 21st-century Solution for Organizations'). Some leaders still pay lip service to supporting greater diversity and the consequences of not hitting target in these areas are not usually significant. The threat of government-enforced quotas may serve to focus minds! I am not a fan of quotas but they will come if organizations don't start addressing the problem themselves.

If organizations genuinely believe that more women on boards is a good thing they must make it easier – by looking at what they mean by flexibility and sending clear messages from the top. Mentoring and development programmes do not work in isolation. In order to solve the problem, CEOs must appoint some women to send clear, visible messages and to become role models themselves.

The women themselves must step up and be ready to take advantage of the opportunities as they present themselves. Self-doubt is not an option. Men and women both have needs and Executive Gremlins. Whilst they manifest for men in unhelpful ways relating to risk and for both in strategy derailment, women seem to allow them to affect their career progression more than men due to lack of confidence. This is a loss for both the women and for the organizations in which they work.

Women must want it badly enough

I hesitated to write this but there are a lot of women out there who aren't prepared to do what it takes to be on a FTSE 500 company board and make the sacrifices required. Do *all* women really want it all?

CASE STUDY

At dinner recently with a FTSE 500 CEO, he said to me that he didn't think they did. That he would prefer to appoint a new female group director but had yet to find one. He did not agree with targets and wanted to appoint on merit.

CASE STUDY

Another aspiring board director client said to me that she was aware that her career was over now that she had had a baby. Her request to work four days a week for a period of time had been declined and she had been advised that she was lucky she was 'only' expected to work nine to five now. She is contemplating giving up work as it is 'just too hard'.

It is in the deconstruction of our thoughts and emotions that we gain insights. In my experience women are particularly vulnerable to their emotions and allow their fears to affect their self-perception and confidence. It is vital that they learn to handle them better if they are to be successful in larger numbers.

In Figure 6.1 I have summarized leaders' views that support those expressed in this chapter. Their perceptions were that women are not affected more than men by stress but they do talk about it more. They are not perceived to 'stand up and be counted' – they do not push themselves and insist their voices are heard when going for promotions or new roles. Lack of confidence appears to be their number one issue. Most do not believe there is a glass ceiling although they did see that unconscious bias is still a problem.

I encourage other women and organizations to get out there and do what it takes to make a difference. Those that can master their own

FIGURE 6.1

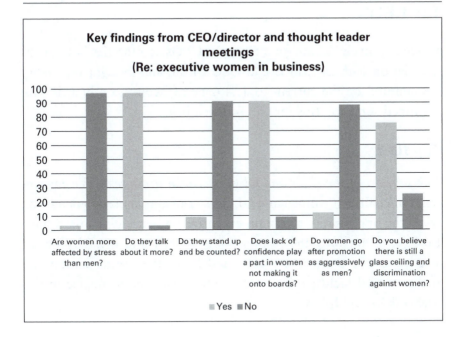

gremlins and understand and help others to master theirs will have an inherent executive advantage. Even if you do not suffer from executive anxiety yourself, you may be aware that some of the women leaders reporting to you do and be at a loss to know what to do with them. The Executive Advantage 10-Step Solution for Resilient 21st-century Leaders will help you!

Organizations must build a pipeline of talented women. They must create a more inclusive culture and solve the problem in a long-term healthy manner of how to get more women on boards. The top-to-bottom thinking involved from thought leadership, events, mentoring, development programmes – all these will help senior women to unlock their potential, navigate organizational politics and improve their performance. In the process they will also improve their networking skills, more effectively manage their careers, their bosses and in some cases their lives. This all takes place working within the framework of the Executive Advantage approach. This is not a quick-fix approach but an in-depth journey of discovery that takes place over several months.

Getting more women on boards – top tips for CEOs

I chaired a lively debate for a group of CEOs at a top tier law firm in association with Critical Eye (a CEO forum and thought leadership community) on the current topical issue of 'Women on boards'. We identified some top tips for CEOs, listed below.

Top tip 1

The support of the chair and CEO is critical to success. The engagement of chairmen/women and CEOs is critical to more women being given the opportunity to obtain executive/non-executive board positions. It is not only the responsibility of HR and diversity heads. Executives are the primary role models for their organization and if they model inclusive leadership, and reward performance in this area, others will follow.

Top tip 2

A shift in thinking at the top is required. Whilst in the past there was perceived to be conscious bias against women in organizations this is no longer the case. Bias is regarded as being unconscious; women are just not 'in the frame' when conversations take place about who might be potential promotion material. A shift in thinking must occur at the top of organizations and women must be prepared to put their heads above the parapet and be noticed. Self-promotion, networking and 'playing the game' were seen as key. There was in fact some debate about playing the game as some felt this was inauthentic. Sector seems to be relevant here. In highly formalized environments such as investment banking, law and top consultancies, there is an element of playing the game required in order to be seen as 'promotable'. However, once a woman has made it to the top, being female may be an advantage as they stand out. In other industries, like IT and telecoms and public sector, it seems to be easier to be different at all levels. Being different registers a threat response in the brain initially.

Top tip 3

Targets or quotas? The question of targets and quotas was discussed and the majority agreed that whilst targets were a good thing, going as far as quotas was 'a step too far'. The findings of the recent Davies Report were consistent with this view. However, there is some sympathy with quotas if things do not start to improve soon. The debate is seen to have gone on long enough. The main reason for not having quotas was that women might be seen as getting there by default rather than merit. It was felt that headhunters need to be more persuasive with reluctant chairmen about introducing more women candidates to shortlists and to be more creative in their searches. It was also felt that headhunters tend to 'heat seek' and that they should be more proactive in their searches for more women, rather than going back to their old networks which tend to be full of men!

Top tip 4

Women should promote more women once on the board. Existing and newly engaged/promoted women should actively promote the appointment of more women to their boards. They have the opportunity to provide exposure and profile for female talent and should use this actively in support. It is important to go beyond a lone female board member as there is a risk that her male colleagues will assume that she is representative of all female views and behaviours and that may not be the case.

Top tip 5

The 80/20 rule. Women still suffer from the '80/20 confidence rule'. Men with 80 per cent of the required skills for a job will see themselves as perfect for the role whereas a woman may focus on the 20 per cent she doesn't have and be open about any lack of experience. Headhunters already know this. So do forward-thinking leaders of organizations, but it is worth remembering when selecting 'the best person for the job'. This is one of the things that fuels unconscious bias.

Top tip 6

Dare to be authentic. Whilst it was acknowledged that in some organizations it was necessary to play the game to some degree on the way up, it was vital that we have more executive role models on boards who were themselves, and not women trying to be men. This was seen as promoting valuable diversity, which has been shown in numerous studies to lead to greater profitability.

Top tip 7

Recommend women for NED positions. When any senior person (male or female) is asked for recommendations for NED positions they should actively promote women and be prepared to take a risk. There was some discussion around 'the same old names' being mentioned as no one wants to take a risk with a new person that no one has heard of. This means that women, who are largely new, are consistently overlooked.

Top tip 8

Women need to network more. Women still don't network in the same way as men. They rarely prioritize a drink with colleagues after work, few play golf or attend sporting events. Organizations need to recognize this and provide opportunities for women to socialize and network by building on each other's experiences. For their part women need to recognize that networking and raising their profile are vital to commercial effectiveness. A board member of a CEO forum commented that it was harder to get women to join Critical Eye than men and has volunteered to promote women more broadly on the website and to consider how to attract more. Whether this is because there are fewer of them or because of an innate reluctance by the women to invest in themselves and network more is unclear. Networks such as An Inspirational Journey, Everywoman, Women in Technology, Women in Business and Finance and lobby group Opportunity Now are all excellent. Networking outside your professional circle can also be useful.

Top tip 9

Women want more flexibility. Although only lightly touched upon in the discussion group, the issue of flexibility, particularly as women are still often primary carers for children and older relatives, is still seen as a major barrier. How can they do it all and still function at board level? Whilst many women want the opportunity, not all women will want to do what is necessary in terms of hours in order to hold a main board director role in a FTSE company.

Top tip 10

Set up mentoring and development programmes. Mentoring programmes are phenomenally successful at helping women to get ahead. A large proportion of the group had benefited from (mainly male) mentors. The lack of female role models at the top of organizations, even when the workforce is predominantly female, is still a problem. Organizations should set aside budget for this if they are serious about gender diversity at the top and women should not wait for formal mentoring programmes but seek out mentors for themselves, even if it is on an informal basis.

Development programmes including executive coaching are also essential to women making the leap onto a board and once they are appointed. If women can identify and learn to handle their Executive Gremlins there will be an increase in confidence and they will have created an executive advantage. If organizations sponsor such programmes (like Merryck & Co, who offer CEO to CEO mentoring for women), they will be well on the way to shifting the needle on the numbers dial of women on boards.

Actions for the individual

- Embrace your Executive Gremlins – don't allow your fears to control you.
- Join networking groups relevant to your stage of career and industry – recognizing that it is often a good thing to network outside your own.

- Work on your confidence and self-beliefs – attend training courses, get a business coach skilled in this area, read. Create some new neural pathways in your brain.

- Lobby your organization to provide access to thought leaders, development programmes, mentors and executive coaching.

- Stand up and be counted! Do some proactive PR!

- Get support if you need it – with admin, with children, with elderly relatives.

In summary, if organizations genuinely believe that more women on boards is a good thing they must make it easier – by sending clear messages from the top. Mentoring and development programmes do not work in isolation. In order to solve the problem, CEOs must appoint some women to send clear, visible messages and they must become inclusive role models and sponsors themselves, creating more inclusive cultures and eliminating unconscious bias. The women themselves must step up and be ready to take advantage of the opportunities as they present themselves. The Executive Advantage 10-Step Solution© will help women to step up. Self-doubt is not an option.

We have explored solutions for organizations specifically for women in this chapter. In Chapter 7, 'The rot starts at the top', we will look at how Executive Gremlins in top leaders cause best laid plans to fail. We will be exploring the wider context of solutions for 21st-century organizations, including authentic flexibility and agility, inclusion and resilience in Chapter 8.

The rot starts at the top

Poor leadership behaviours derail business performance

CASE STUDY

The newly appointed CEO of an IT business was hailed on arrival as the great leader. He was a great guy. Unfortunately, his need to be perceived as 'Important' led to some poor recruitment decisions at the top. The vision was unachievable and his lack of track record in this industry began to show. He lost the confidence of the group board and the people within the company and ultimately the business was taken over. His unaddressed Executive Gremlin or need to feel Important led him to withdraw and he left the company. This negatively affected his leadership team who had enjoyed working for him and this destabilized the business further.

Most recognized leadership 'experts' would support the proposition that 'the rot starts at the top'. When something goes wrong in a business the leaders are blamed. Perhaps this is as it should be, if judged from the perspective of the kudos, status and money that leaders acquire when things are going well. To avoid this situation, businesses need to accept responsibility for executive anxiety caused by relentless 21st-century issues. In the same way as the army sends officers on a tour of duty in dangerous war zones, then gives them a desk job for a year or a less front-line role, organizations should stop expecting their leaders just to deal with these pressures day in day out for years. Whilst some resilient leaders do cope well with the pressure, organizations must recognize that some will need down time and not view this as a career-inhibiting need. Contracts should include down time and sabbaticals with flexibility for people to take time out if they need it after particularly busy times. In this way they would avoid the burnout of key executives that costs them millions of pounds and wipes more off their share value. Businesses today need more authentic leaders and a pipeline of aspiring talent. Fostering this requires board-level commitment, mentoring programmes and visible role models displaying positive leadership behaviours. The rot may start at the top but positive role models can, and should, start there too.

100 per cent of leaders interviewed for this book said that visible leadership was the most critical factor in business success.

" *It is extraordinarily important. Change management is visible leadership in the front line. Historically technical solutions were sought over people solutions. Active engagement is necessary.*

CEO, global FTSE 500

My experience of working with leaders, in both one-to-one coaching and offsite experiential workshops, supports this. If the leaders are charismatic, respected, well regarded and admired, they become trusted and workforce engagement results. I sometimes run an exercise where leaders have to vote on whether a well-known leader is authentic, inauthentic or whether they are trusted. Many of the leaders shown have character flaws yet they are still admired and generally trusted. There is an innate confidence and lack of obvious weakness as far as their 'followers' are concerned. Many famous politicians and world leaders have had affairs, others have 'rolled' a number of companies before making their millions in another, yet overall they are still trusted. Equally, when trust is lost there is no mercy and followers will quickly turn away. This happens in the same way in corporations.

Authenticity and storytelling

One uses stories not because they are true or even because they are false but for the same reason that people tell and listen to them, in order to learn about the terms on which others make sense of their lives.

Brodkey 1987

Inspirational leaders draw rich pictures. They are able to describe future visions in compelling ways and draw on their experiences of the past to tell powerful stories and connect with their people.

Stories can help business leaders connect their people to strategy, vision, values and change. They rouse our minds to add action to feeling. We remember stories about:

- the first man on the moon;
- the wives of Henry VIII;
- Nelson Mandela and Mother Teresa;
- famous battles;
- sporting legends;
- Live Aid and Comic Relief;
- 9/11;
- Barack Obama – 'All things are possible.'

Companies have their own stories that people remember.

Authenticity through storytelling is essentially a search for new meanings. It is concerned with personal journey and learning from experience and translating that into useful information for others. It has been used for generations to communicate messages around the world. It is the stuff of legends and heroes. Storytelling in organizations is a powerful way for leaders to authentically convey their experience in a given situation and to communicate messages disseminated from above to their people below. By reviewing their leadership experiences and using different storytelling approaches, it can drive customer centricity, authenticity and innovation.

Great leaders have stories to tell which can change and build businesses to make great things happen.

Through reflection and incisive questioning, and The Executive Advantage 10-Step Solution©, leaders can learn to explore their own inner worlds and discover new meanings. The value of authenticity and personal disclosure using storytelling by a leader works astonishingly well in the creation of engagement amongst a workforce.

> The choice and use of strategies will depend on the subject under discussion, the occasion and the speaker's identity or deemed role at a particular occasion.
>
> **Aristotle, 350 BC, cited in *Nichomachean Ethics* (1998)**

Personal narrative in all its forms has been talked about since Aristotle (4th century BC), who went on to teach Alexander the Great, whose compelling story was told in many movies and biographies, including the well known leadership book *Are Leaders Born or Are They Made?* by Kets de Vries and Danny (2004).

By allowing leaders and their people to make sense of their shared experience it is possible to facilitate innovation and an improvement in customer centricity.

Encouraging leaders to use storytelling requires them to suspend normal ways of thinking about leadership. It is challenging to some as it is unfamiliar and yet, once they understand, they will often become advocates.

> The stories that were successful for me all had certain characteristics. They were stories that were told from the perspective of a single protagonist who was in a predicament that was prototypical of the organization's business.
>
> **Stephen Denning, The Society for Storytelling**

Business transformations succeed or fail on the strength of decisions and choices made by organizations' leaders. It is leaders' choices that determine who they are and who they will become. If they communicate their personal experience authentically and 'walk the talk', they will engage their people. A story enables a leap in understanding by the audience so as to grasp how an organization or community or complex system may change for the better.

Have you observed leaders who talk about values but don't 'walk the talk'?

CASE STUDY

In the client organization where the MD of one part of the business had lost credibility, with her board and with the group board and non-executive directors, she was perceived as not walking the talk. She was perceived to be unprepared, chaotic and a poor listener. If someone disagreed she would talk more loudly. She was also a really nice person – people liked her but didn't respect her. She had several strategic gremlins – 'Not good enough', which led her to avoid things she didn't feel she was good at, and 'Unlovable', which led to her revisiting the point over and over in order to convince people of her point of view and to spending far too much time talking late into the night in the bar! She felt so under threat that she would micro manage and hound her perfectly capable leaders instead of setting clear strategies and goals and measuring their success against them. These behaviours did not add to her credibility. Despite poor sales results she continued to operate as she always had and was unable to 'up her game'. She was ultimately removed from the business. From her point of view, this came out of the blue, she had no idea why, whereas the board felt they had given feedback on numerous occasions but it had not been listened to.

I have come across this so many times in business. I have sat in numerous presentations where leaders spout forth about their values, then leave the room to go back to bullying their people, or behaving in some other inappropriate way.

> *In times of trouble, values go out of the window.*

Director, IT company

> *Our company's values were held up and often repeated in leadership programmes but it was not really a meritocracy and integrity was challenged during the credit crunch.*
>
> **Global director, financial services organization**

Respondents to interview questions for this book said they had experienced this and most gave specific examples. Several described CEOs who took all the credit but left others to do all the work. This is particularly important when considering the whole area of inclusivity as a key capability for 21st-century leadership – will emotionally immature leaders continue to pay lip service to the inclusion of more women and other minority groups on boards or will they actually change their existing mindsets?

> *He was a Champagne Charlie with a budget of billions who spent all his time going to awards ceremonies and lunches. He was a flake but there was a process behind him and the team did all the work so it wasn't visible.*
>
> **Public sector director**

> *We have a CEO who tries and says he is a 'people person' but is the least 'people person' I have ever met!*
>
> **Anonymous**

Factions and mafias

In the example above where there was a faction that wanted the MD to go, they did not rate her performance, and their opinions were instrumental in the final outcome. As individuals in this group there was strong trust and interdependency and group think.

Many organizations suffer from factions and mafias, small powerful groups within an organization that tend to share common expectations and have the same political agendas.

> *In M&A this is the thing that destroys value. There is always an acquirer, the target retrenches and battles for survival. There are fights for roles and control. It is a 'collective powerless' thing.*
>
> **Jeremy Small, group company secretary, AXA UK plc**

They display hostile behaviours when faced with interlopers or perceived outsiders, especially if they come with new ideas and expectations requiring them to change. They will often succeed in undermining new people who join a team and damage their credibility. They can become entrenched geographically – people talk of north–south divides – and also organizationally, for example where there is conflict between head office strategy functions and line management. Leaders should be aware and conscious of any group think on their boards and leadership teams and take positive steps towards greater diversity of person and thought. Individuals should be encouraged to take a risk and think outside the box. Group think comes about when individuals believe they know the answers based on their experiences of the past and their consequent strong mental maps and belief systems. Executive Gremlins build together to form beliefs that can be shared. Whilst in some cases this can be a good thing, in the case of prejudice it is obviously not.

Underperforming boards, leadership teams and individual board members

I was part of an MBO team which was built from scratch and intensive work was put in to have a great team who were all well rewarded. The NEDs commented on how strong a team we had and much was made of this in the flotation prospectus.

Successful businesses tend to have emotionally mature, well-balanced boards and leadership teams. Trust and mutual respect are prevalent. In underperforming businesses the opposite usually holds true.

When change programmes do not go well, the performance of the leaders is usually in question. Poor performance and bad decision making almost always come about as a result of Executive Gremlins being in charge. As you have already seen in earlier chapters, the brain's response to negative beliefs and stress triggers is that the prefrontal cortex shuts down and the amygdala takes over because it perceives a threat. The resulting behaviour is sometimes known colloquially as 'the lights are on but no one's home'. I have observed some companies where the board paid lip service to each other but did not support board decisions in the wider areas of the business. In others, diversity on boards was not encouraged and group think prevailed.

Off target!

Quarterly targets are obsessively driven.

MD, global IT company

CASE STUDY

I worked with another sales director who had been with his company for a long time and who had helped build the business from scratch. The CEO was critical as they were not growing the business but the sales director felt that they were ahead of their competitors and therefore doing well in a difficult marketplace. (They sold financial software to investment banks – the period in question was just post credit crunch.) His Executive Gremlins included a 'Not good enough' fear. The more the current CEO pushed him and provided evidence of his non-performance, the more paralyzed and demoralized my client became. Even when he obtained a huge order he found it hard to celebrate his success as it went so far against his belief system to feel that way. Not being good enough was more familiar. His lack of self-belief caused by this led to him being unassertive and lacking in presence in meetings. We worked on this and the CEO recognized that he was becoming more assertive, his sales performance improved, and he was perceived as being more successful as a result.

I have been called in to work with a number of sales directors and CEOs whose businesses were off target. I listen to them, and to others in forums and networking events. They fear the quarterly targets. Shareholder expectations have become very short term with most wanting to see tangible ROI in a very short space of time. This exacerbates executive anxiety and often works against leaders feeling and being successful.

> *Quarterly targets are massively important. Individual targets are tied to it.*
> *I have been personally conflicted between the short and long term.*
>
> **Global director**

Ninety-eight per cent of private sector company interview respondents recognized the pressure around targets, though not all were quarterly driven. Public sector leaders spoke of making targets in order to focus minds and increase productivity. Targets were largely accepted as being necessary evils although several respondents spoke of being internally conflicted between making short-term gains against long-term profitability in order to meet shareholder expectations. Most expressed the view that US companies were obsessively driven around quarters and spoke of their own companies as having the right amount of pressure compared to, for example, Enron.

> *You have to pick your battles re signings, revenue and profit. You should*
> *be able to work out how or work somewhere else!*
>
> **Vice President, global IT company**

The investment in improving leadership behaviours and performance is worth it

Whether good leaders are born or made, most need some sort of help along the way. Whether this takes the form of formal leadership training, formal or informal mentoring or executive coaching, most successful organizations make a substantial investment in an improvement in leadership behaviours and capability, with varying results. This investment is even more important in preparing leaders for 21st-century leadership as a shift in thinking is required. The world of business is no longer the same. Most leading-edge business schools now have forward-thinking programmes around authenticity and 'being real', being willing to show the leader's human side and improving emotional intelligence. One of the key ways of changing the sort of mindsets that still lead to the perception or reality of discrimination is to train leaders in inclusive leadership, and to make the business case for diversity at the very top. Being resilient is an important component of this and a vital component of 21st-century leadership in general. If The Executive Advantage 10-Step Solution were to be on every leadership curriculum we would soon have organizations full of resilient 21st-century leaders. Very few leaders interviewed had specific programmes for operational boards or above and those that did not focus on resilience, handling pressure or inclusion. Leadership programmes in organizations vary from very technical to very behavioural (that is, addressing the 'inner human' in the leadership role). The Executive Advantage programme addresses the behavioural side of leadership but very firmly in the context of the organization rather than just as a piece of new theory.

My team and I have been working with leaders via behavioural programmes, providing mentoring and executive coaching, for over 20 years. Our most successful clients committed fully to the process. We would link leadership development to real projects in the business and evaluate progress, conduct 360s, hold regular offsites and support with executive coaching. We started at the top and involved leaders at all levels in the process.

We always include work on executive anxiety and Executive Gremlins. These sessions elicit the most favourable feedback as people realize (gladly) that they are not alone and that understanding this work gives them a significant executive advantage.

FIGURE 7.1

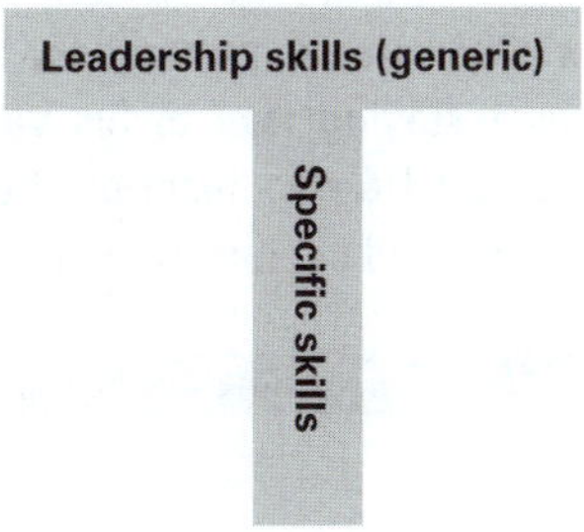

CASE STUDY

I worked with a very successful subsidiary of a large telecoms company, who coined the phrase 'The T-shaped professional' where leaders had to have consistent leadership understanding, values and behaviours across the top of the T, with significant technical depth in their specialist subject forming the downward element. People were not promoted only for being brilliant technical operators, they had to demonstrate consistent leadership as well. This was linked to pay and performance mechanisms within the business. The net result was that poor performers were identified and given appropriate help and the organization was able to transform to a project-based environment. Bid teams and project teams came together seamlessly and politics and factions were minimized as leaders were focused on the task rather than individuals' egos. We ran programmes which were developed to support critical players and top talent groups in support of this.

Think longer term and bigger picture

CASE STUDY

Bill George, ex CEO of Medtronic and now a Harvard professor, discusses this in his excellent book *Authentic Leadership – Rediscovering the Secrets of Creating Lasting Value* (Jossey Bass 2003). He describes how he made tough decisions, and grew his business, whilst staying true to his values and beliefs, without compromising to make the quarter. He also describes how his first marriage failed and how he is a much better husband second time around!

I often hear business leaders complain about their shareholder expectations. The pressure to perform quarter on quarter, year on year is relentless and makes long-term decision making more difficult.

How does pressure affect leadership behaviours, good and bad? Are leaders conflicted?

> *[The stress of] regulators keeping changing their minds – it causes distrust and lack of bravery.*
>
> **CEO**

Leaders' responses to this question suggested that pressure affects people quite individually. Some thrive on it and others get extremely stressed. They said that some people were conflicted about doing what's right for the long term versus making the short-term win.

> *There was some less favourable behaviour during the financial crisis and people were taking short-term decisions. I felt conflicted but stood my ground and refused to liquidate $60 million stock. It was the right decision but it could have led to me losing my job.*
>
> **CEO**

CASE STUDY

A chairman I know of a telecoms plc took on the executive leadership role in an underperforming company only if his shareholders accepted that there would be an upward trend on business results in the first two years rather than a set figure as it was impossible to predict how markets would react in the credit crunch. By doing this he was able to give his leadership team flexibility in sales and marketing. In year one they were able to improve performance largely by improvements in efficiency and cutting wastage, which then left year two to focus on sales transformation and growth. Whilst he was not particularly happy with the speed of ramping up, he was able to paint a positive picture to his shareholders and the market and the company's share price was not compromised; in fact it improved.

Had he agreed to arbitrary numbers and failed to hit them, confidence would have been negatively affected. Had the share price dropped, shareholder pressure would have increased. This would in turn have led to a crisis in leadership confidence and leaders being controlled by their anxieties. General disengagement of the workforce would follow, making growth even more difficult to achieve and causing a downward spiral.

Leaders must be willing to take personal risks

I was working as a consultant for an IT company when the CEO decided to undertake an MBO with a couple of his directors. They asked me to join them. Whilst they were comfortable with me working for both companies, the original company was not and forced me to choose. The start-up was obviously the riskier option as it was tiny by comparison but the team was strong with a great vision so I went with them. I also chose them because I felt valuable working for them (my relatedness need). However, it was still a risk. We successfully floated the company in three years and several directors retired!

I nearly lost my job for refusing to compromise my authenticity. I was asked to skew my results and I refused.

Global director, financial services

Leaders at times must be prepared to take a personal risk, to allow people to see who they really are and to be willing at times to be unpopular. Authenticity is a vital component in credible 21st-century leadership. Top leaders are role models and mentors for the organization. What they stand for and how they operate are scrutinized by employees and the marketplace, particularly in a plc. The balance between presenting a professional image and being real is key to success. Too much image and people won't trust you, too little and you are in danger of losing respect. Similarly, being willing to show who you are is a strength, whilst running out your problems can create uncertainty and fear. This is why C-suite development is so important. Often boards are overlooked when it comes to executive development programmes, which are typically focused further down the organization. Having made it, it is assumed they know everything they need to know. In fact, many leaders have had very narrow careers and may have been promoted for results like sales or other expertise rather than their leadership abilities. Top-level development is often conducted one to one via executive coaching or at expensive offsites with business schools. The best programmes tend to focus on the 'being' side of leadership rather than on skills development. They foster the development of the whole person and encourage authenticity and sharing of experience. The dilemma of sharing just enough, whilst remaining professional and credible, is very real.

CEOs and leaders at the top of organizations have often reported that the most valuable part of their coaching with me, or in offsite workshops with their teams, is having a 'safe place to share' as it is inappropriate to use their shareholders or their direct reports as sounding boards. The increased focus on managing corporate risk makes this especially tough, especially since the banking crisis which rocked the financial institutions and everyone in the food chain beyond them. As previously mentioned, newspaper reports at the time of this banking crisis, and CEO forums that I have attended since, have suggested that if there had been more women on investment banks' boards they would not have taken so many risks since women are perceived as more risk averse. They are also perceived as more willing to share; neuroscience and my research for this book support this view. Testosterone is found to promote risk taking and men have ten times as much as women. Women are more affected by high levels of cortisol, the stress hormone, and are more likely to work more collaboratively.

Companies and individuals are constantly balancing risk versus gain. Leaders must be prepared to jump off the cliff sometimes and go for it. I have done this many times in my career and sometimes they have paid off and other times they haven't.

Risk

Generally, organizations use up a lot of leader hours ticking boxes for their risk management systems. It's important to actually change the risk profile of your business – the system should be a management tool, not all about compliance.

FTSE 500 director

Have you ever taken a personal risk rather than compromise your authenticity?

100 per cent said they wouldn't compromise their authenticity and gave examples of when they largely said 'no' to doing things that felt wrong. They described this as incredibly stressful.

I left a top-tier consultancy when I felt a partner had crossed a line. He sold a project to a client for £20 million when a £2 million project would have done the job. I felt it was important to stay outside the grey zone.

Global MD, IT

Leaders also learn to take personal risks with regard to their relationships. We are products of our early experiences and these shape how we see the world. Our perceptions create filters, which affect our willingness to take risks. We make sacrifices along the way. We sometimes have to take risks when it comes to our family and our work colleagues. What seems to be true is that the less defended we are, the better our relationships. If we allow ourselves to notice our fears without judgement, to observe them and move on, rather than overreacting and blowing things out of proportion, we will ultimately be more successful as people and business leaders. Mindfulness training is particularly helpful to some people wanting to learn how to do this.

The bottom line with regard to managing risk for 21st-century leaders is that leaders are also human beings – in many cases 'human doings' that distract themselves from who they are and what is important by keeping busy 'doing things'. Human beings have needs that must be met, and Executive Gremlins, if left unaddressed, will grow until they are buttons the size of satellite dishes! As we have seen in earlier chapters, these cause us to overreact to external stimuli. Executives become so oversensitive they cease to make rational decisions. They react to the stimuli based on their preconditioned beliefs and pre-existing patterns in their brains. Strong emotionally mature leaders are able to put their own anxiety to one side, to focus on the job in hand. They also recognize that others may need a little help to get there. The investment in supporting, challenging and developing leaders is therefore worth it. The Executive Advantage solutions for organizations are a vital component.

I interviewed leaders at the top of their game in order to test the validity of my thinking. I asked questions that relate to my research for the development of the Executive Advantage solutions outlined in this book. I was excited to discover that they largely agreed with my theories and point of view about needs, stress and leadership and the impact this has. Indeed, some of those interviewed were struggling to know what to do about these issues. The next sections are a summary of what they told me.

Key elements

- 75 per cent of the research interviews clearly showed that the majority of leaders in top positions today, across all sectors, concurred that executive anxiety is a major derailer of performance and therefore affects the success of large-scale business change programmes.

- 100 per cent of leaders felt that visible leadership was crucial to business success.

- Most had experienced feeling Unimportant, Unlovable, Out of Control, Not good enough, Stupid or Powerless.

- Most had experienced working with negative leadership styles and almost all related to bullying.

- All but one had experienced times in their careers where they had been extremely stressed to the point of affecting their ability to think.

- 98 per cent admitted to having misread situations due to preconceived beliefs.

Organizational investment

- Invest in leadership development even when you have to downsize. It is when you need resilient 21st-century leaders the most.

- Include modules on resilience – The Executive Advantage 10-Step Solution for Resilient 21st-century Leaders©.

- Provide positive mentors and role models.

- Identify critical elements of 21st-century leadership for your business. Make it culturally OK for leaders to be different and for leaders to admit when they need time out.

In this chapter we have explored how the rot starts at the top and how vital it is to ensure your top leaders understand what is required of them – to walk the talk, be authentic, manage risk and generally be resilient 21st-century leaders. Since writing this chapter, I have become aware of some research which says that successful CEOs do not tend to suffer stress. If this is true they certainly recognize periods in their careers when they have done. Also, the term 'successful' may have something to do with this as stress does not tend to lead to success! In the final chapter I provide an overview of the 21st-century Leadership Solutions for Organizations, which include the three leadership capabilities: authentic flexibility and agility, inclusion and resilience.

The Executive Advantage 21st-century Solution for Organizations

Key trends for 21st-century leadership

The key global concerns deserving of consideration by 21st-century leaders are energy, population explosion and consequent shifts in world power and technology. Handling the resulting increased complexity, relentless change, pace and cultural implications has created the need for a new set of behavioural competencies for all leaders, over and above those needed to do the day job. These are authentic flexibility and agility, inclusivity and resilience. This book is mainly about the third element, resilience. If leaders can learn to manage their own Executive Gremlins, and organizations put in place processes and practices that support these competencies, then a culture shift will occur. It is my vision that all business schools and large organizations with leadership programmes will one day include training on resilience and specifically the 10-Step Solution. It may sound cheesy and overused but I actually do want to make a difference and the only way I know how is through improving leaders' behaviour in organizations as this will have a knock-on effect, touching many more people positively than I could reach alone.

FIGURE 8.1

Key 21st-century behavioural capabilities

Recognized thought leaders have been talking about authenticity for years. Authentic leadership is basically the need for leaders to be real and congruent, to have vision and to communicate in ways that engage and build trust in their organizations. It is not just about looking like the leaders that have gone before – though some organizations still recruit and train people in this way. Organizations must learn to look beyond their mental maps of success and seek out people who can be flexible, inclusive and resilient in the face of challenging market conditions and constant world change. Twenty-first-century leadership is not about leadership 'nice to haves' but rather about commercial imperatives that will deliver profitability. It has become an imperative because of societal changes.

Loss of meaning

A sense of meaning is no longer provided for leaders by their families or by organizations. When people worked their whole lives for one company, they were loyal and in most cases the company looked after them. Traditional families with a mother, father and 2.4 children are less common than they used to be. These days it is important to formalize purpose and visions to help people to understand where they fit in. Things like performance appraisal, although sometimes arduous for the busy executive, help people understand how they are doing and adjustments can be made.

Loss of community

The growth of global organizations and speed of communication have led to people working in virtual teams and global markets. There is a loss of community inherent in this. People like to sit next to their colleagues. As companies grow, shared experience is important to engage people. This accounts for the increased demand for training in storytelling for executives.

Employees are more cynical than they used to be

Things must be proved rather than just accepted. Children no longer automatically respect adults and teachers. There is a sense of 'we've heard it all before'. This is particularly true of companies where cost cutting and redundancies are the order of the day. Providing vision and direction via authentic communication works much better than 'boxed communication'. I have worked for several of the biggest communications companies in the world. One is particularly inauthentic. The turnover of senior leadership means that the workforce is particularly cynical when yet another new CEO turns up and tells them how great the future is looking!

We all know and accept now that it is important to create a compelling vision and to explore values, to implement forward-thinking culture and communication programmes and to devise key performance indicators (KPIs) and goals for employees at all levels. We know that 'people strategies' and authentic leadership development are important. However, there are some key capabilities emerging for 21st-century leaders that go beyond these. The most successful 21st-century leaders are able to manage across matrix structures and adapt their behaviour according to geographic area, organizational culture and individual circumstance. To succeed in the new landscape, leaders must rethink their attitudes and beliefs and organizations must build key capabilities in the following areas.

Authentic flexibility and agility

FIGURE 8.2

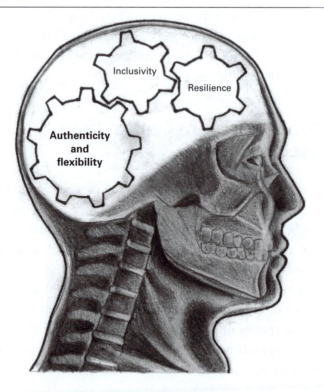

I am often asked by leaders of organizations seeking to grow, 'How do I create a more agile organization?' There is a consciousness that it is necessary but a lack of understanding of how to get there. There is a whole variety of answers but they basically come down to culture: giving people permission to be agile and flexible. This sounds simple but it isn't. In highly controlled environments where managing risk and corporate governance is the order of the day, allowing people the freedom to act and the flexibility to do things their own way can be fraught with scary consequences. There is a delicate balance required. I remember back in the early 90s lots of people were talking about KPIs and SIPs (strategic implementation plans). They are perhaps even more important today than they were then. In 21st-century leadership situations it is important that employees are focused at all levels on outcomes rather than detail, that people are allowed the flexibility and autonomy to decide the journey they take to their ultimate destinations. They deal with the 'what' rather than the 'how'. Systems and processes must be designed to support flexibility and agility rather than hinder them. This means cutting levels of reporting and sign-off. It requires entrepreneurs to become more systematic and the control leaders to become more flexible and to let go. Only by exploring this will the levels of each be identified for your business. For example, in the highly regulated world of investment banking, flexibility will mean different things to different types of business, be they an IT or telecoms business or a more creative organization. Global businesses must look at what flexibility will look like in each country, as perceptions of freedom to act will vary around the world. Having leaders on the ground that understand the territory is especially important to agility. Having clear boundaries and deliverables enables both risk management and agility.

Practical steps

Step 1: Define the culture you want

The culture should support the business you are trying to be. Hold regular offsites and thinking environments – success is achieved not only by working harder.

Step 2: Think about agility and flexibility by region

Appropriate freedom to act will be very different in Japan, Saudi Arabia, Africa, the USA and Russia! One size will not fit all.

Step 3: Simplify performance management systems

Ensure they support agility and flexibility – think KPI, not detailed appraisals and systems for their own sake.

Step 4: Link leadership pay to cultural performance as well as financial performance

One will impact the other.

Inclusivity

FIGURE 8.3

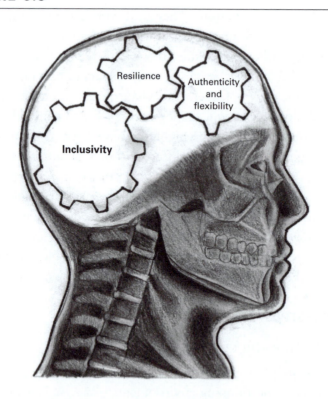

The demands of 21st-century leadership have pushed inclusion up the agenda. The emergence of China and India as the future super-powers means we must embrace difference or be left behind. Whilst there is difference between and within Europe and the USA, there are more differences between East and West, differences that cannot be ignored. Talent will no longer be found in the same places. Universities and business schools in Europe are already struggling to cope with the demand for places from these countries and they are setting up their own 'super universities'. Ignoring this shift and assuming organizations will look the same in terms of board composition, with business plans that suit Western cultures, are not an option.

> *New research into inclusive leadership started from the knowledge that making the most of a diverse workforce is not just the right thing to do, it is a commercial imperative.*
>
> **Opportunity Now report, September 2011**

Organizations are realizing that the world of work is no longer the same. Old-style hierarchical structures are no longer suitable frame-works for managing change and workforces are becoming more diverse. Inclusive leaders are critical to act as role models for organizational diversity. They create environments where women and other groups recognized as 'diverse' can thrive, and where strong talent pipelines can produce diverse boards that are more representative of the organizations they lead. For example, as mentioned in Chapter 6, the publication of the Davies Report in 2011 set targets for chairs and CEOs to increase the numbers of women on boards. At the six-month mark they had made progress but not hit these targets. A year on, little had changed. The fear of quotas is high. If we are to really fix this problem, women need to step up and current leaders must become more inclusive, not just by paying lip service to the problem but also by their actions day to day in their own organizations, by being inclusive of gender, race, disability, and sexual orientation. Any level of leader from CEO to line manager may be inclusive. Their impact may be much larger than their notional status. Currently pioneers, these leaders are learning to be inclusive on the job. They are inherently open-minded but they are still not being developed as part of mainstream organizational programmes.

In order to develop inclusive leaders in organizations it is important to understand what they are. They tend to have a unique blend of knowledge, skills and behaviours which lead to tangible actions. They understand how to build diverse teams and flex their own styles, to communicate and coach. They are role models and build inclusive cultures. They have high trust levels and genuinely respect others. They are consistent, authentic, provide visible sponsorship and help people at an individual level to succeed. They seek to influence decision makers on the importance of diversity and inclusion.

Inclusive leadership fosters employee engagement and they become more productive as a result. Opportunity Now research found the following:

> *Eighty per cent of employees who had experienced an inclusive leader reported that this leader successfully increased their motivation, loyalty and performance and made them more likely to go the extra mile.*

So how do we encourage inclusive leadership?

Five-step framework for mainstreaming inclusion as a core leadership capability:

Practical steps

Step 1: Define the strategic imperative for your business

The strategic imperative for inclusive leadership is that businesses with inclusive cultures have been shown to be more profitable. This is true even in sectors where the mantra has become 'getting more for less'. The credit-crunch cuts have demoralized and demotivated people working in organizations at all levels. Inclusive leadership will help. Many organizations are still led by white, middle-class,

FIGURE 8.4

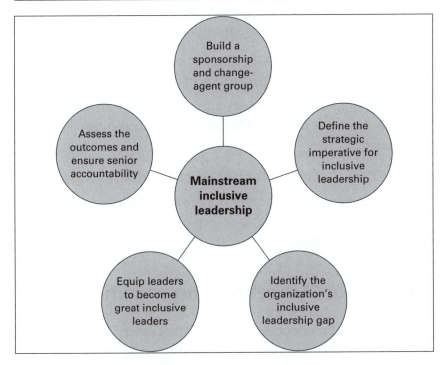

SOURCE: Shapiro, G (2011) Executive summary, *Opportunity Now: Inclusive Leadership – from Pioneer to Mainstream*, Business in the Community, London

middle-aged men. This has got to change and it will change only if the issue of pipeline is addressed. Happy, motivated staff will improve customer service and ultimately productivity. Inclusive leadership works, at every level, in any type of organization. It is important that the strategic imperative is identified for your own organization, not organizations in general.

Step 2: Identify your organization's inclusive leadership gap

The gap is the area identified as needing work. For many organizations the hot topic is getting more women on boards. It could equally be recruiting say, more leaders locally in China and ensuring their fit with the global organization to encourage growth. Identifying non-executive directors that reflect this gap may be a good start.

Step 3: Train leaders to become more inclusive

Implement forward-thinking programmes and allow talented people to work in different cultures from early in their careers.

Step 4: Ensure success is measured and leaders rewarded against performance in being inclusive

Ensure board-level commitment – this starts by identifying the strategic imperative for doing it. There needs to be a commercial reason for bothering.

Step 5: Build a sponsorship and change-agent group

Allow them freedom to act and opportunities to present their successes at the highest levels. Give exposure to young leaders with enthusiasm and passion.

Support for 21st-century organizations

We have seen the importance of the 21st-century leadership capabilities of authentic flexibility and agility, inclusion and resilience. In this section I show what is required in terms of support:

- thought leadership;
- mentoring;
- development.

Thought leadership

Governments need to provide funding and encourage lobby groups to produce new information about 21st-century leadership capabilities, publishing papers and articles that reach a wide audience, and business schools should start incorporating modules on their executive leadership programmes and MBAs. The subject of resilience is so critical they should make it a compulsory element. Large organizations should commission training and development programmes that include these too. They must also provide role models and reward those who demonstrate the behaviours and strategies that work. Internally, companies should set up sponsorship, mentoring and

FIGURE 8.5

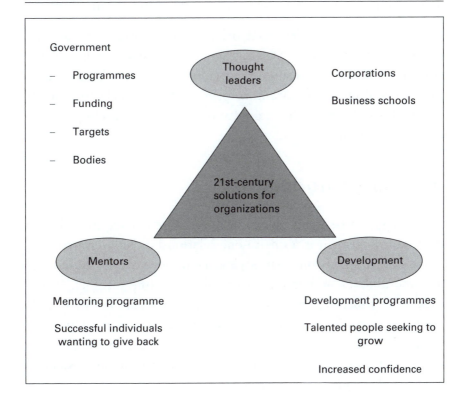

development programmes and encourage benchmarking with other organizations and bodies.

Mentoring in organizations

The commitment of leaders across organizations is vital to the success of any change programme and perhaps especially so in programmes attempting to transition the organization to a resilient, inclusive, flexible 21st-century culture. If mentoring has the visible support of the chair and the CEO, the rest of the organization will get on board. Relegate it to an HR initiative and it will never have the same impact, however talented the HR leader. How many CEOs know how to create a culture shift in their organization? How many HR leaders, often seeking board appointments themselves, are able to truly facilitate this type of change at the level required? Mentoring programmes help talented young leaders gain informal sponsorship and become role models for younger people seeking promotion.

Leaders need to consider what behaviours are acceptable in their organizations. In terms of programmes, the best single thing a company can do to transition their culture long term is to set up a mentoring programme. Mentors provide role models for success and build confidence. They can also open doors and help people to network more successfully.

What is mentoring?

Mentoring can be many things in many different scenarios but in its broadest terms it is a one-to-one relationship between two individuals based simply on the needs and aspirations of one (the mentee) and the abilities and resources of the other (the mentor). It is a process in which one person oversees the career of another outside the manager–subordinate relationship. It is a protected relationship in which learning and experimentation can occur, potential skills can be developed and results can be measured over time. Mentors are trusted friends and supporters.

The term 'mentor' was first used by Homer in *The Odyssey*. Ulysses left his trusted friend Mentor in charge of his household and son Telemachus whilst he was away fighting in the Trojan War. Mentor largely failed in his duties but the goddess Pallas Athene stepped in and helped Telemachus in a number of disguises. Disguised as Mentor, she acted as a wise and trusted advisor and counsellor helping him grow in experience, maturity and courage.

Mentoring may be differentiated from other forms of developmental interventions in that it is not typically goal focused, which is more often the case in executive coaching, nor does it attempt to educate via skills development as in leadership training programmes. It is most appropriate to protégés seeking role models, sounding boards and advisors whose opinions they rate and who have typically 'been there' and 'done that'. It is not, as is sometimes supposed, a very senior coach or line manager, though it will certainly cohabit the same territory! The learning agenda stays with the protégé. The mentor guides, encourages, advises, teaches, inspires, challenges and corrects without criticizing.

When it comes to mentoring, the metaphor of the family is useful. In a fully functioning family there is the child, the parent(s) and the grandparents or other relatives who provide informal support. The child is naturally inquisitive and wants to learn. The parents are responsible for setting boundaries and expectations, encouraging positive goals and monitoring their progress in action. The grandparents, uncles and aunts act as mentors and provide a different but equally valuable function. They typically have years of experience and because they are not involved in the day-to-day functioning of the family, they have distance and perspective. They can give advice that would not be taken from a parent. They enrich the development of the protégé.

So, if we apply this metaphor to organizations, the protégé is the person being mentored, they are responsible for their own self-managed learning. The parent equivalent is the line manager, responsible for setting goals, monitoring performance and coaching the protégé within an organization. The mentor is the 'wise old uncle' whose advice is greatly valued and whose knowledge and experience are in great demand. Mentors are typically (though not always) older and senior to the learner, and they are secure in their own positions. They are long serving in their own (not necessary the same) organizations and have access to resources and information.

The benefits of mentoring for mentors

- high degree of personal fulfilment;
- opportunity to shape rising stars;
- personal learning through experience and challenge from mentee;
- experience of managing performance in a different way.

Qualities of a good mentor

- good motivator, perceptive, able to support mentoring objectives;
- high performer, secure in their own position;
- older and usually senior to the learner, more knowledgeable;
- able to advise and instruct without interfering;
- sees mentoring as a way of 'giving back'.

The benefits of mentoring for mentees

- It is a protected relationship, not specifically focused on an organization.
- There is greater clarity around career development.
- There are accelerated learning opportunities.
- An experienced and confidential sounding board to bounce ideas off.
- Help with preparation for formal evaluation/interviews.
- Acknowledgement and acceptance – builds confidence.
- Focus on career development, not operational objectives.
- One to one: 'two minds and one agenda'.
- Fast-track career progression.
- Helps mentee to create supportive networks, inside and outside the organization.

Mentoring is traditionally longer term and more informal than other forms of development. Many of the skills required to be a good coach will also apply in mentoring, for instance questioning, listening, being a safe place to share. An effective mentoring relationship often results in learning for both parties. For example, in gender-based mentoring, male mentors often learn about the female experience in corporations whilst helping the career of the woman.

I hope my daughters don't have to go through what my mentees go through when they eventually start work.

Global finance director, IT company

Whilst always being committed to the promotion of women in theory, in practice it made much more impact when he thought about it as a result of actually mentoring a woman in his own organization in a personal way.

Clutterbuck, who is often regarded as the guru of mentoring, believes that anyone can be a mentor if they have information of value and the skills and time to do it. He cites the benefits to organizations as improvement in retention, succession planning, change management and engagement. Most forward-thinking organizations have some form of mentoring programme, although these are often targeted at graduates and in some cases schools. Mentoring should occur at all levels.

Development

If companies are serious about preparing leaders for 21st-century leadership and cultural redesign to meet the new economic realities they must invest in leadership development programmes at all levels. Starting with the board, they must discuss what sort of organizations they want to be. Executive programmes should include modules on authenticity, flexibility, inclusion and resilience, especially resilience, as leaders will not be able to do any of the former if they burn out! Too many companies roll out expensive 'same old, same old' programmes that they have run for years. With increased emphasis on leadership, development spend should be focused on behavioural change, rather than technical know-how and methodology. Facilitated 'white space' thinking forums should be held regularly, rather than prescriptive programmes where experts 'know' the solutions for your leaders. Expert facilitators and thinkers should prepare to 'hold the space' using a toolkit of experience to go with the group and allow them to explore what is right for their business.

TABLE 8.1

Key stages of successful mentoring programmes	Steps to take
They are sponsored at the highest level.	Communicate with separately, encourage commitment from mentors, and emphasize importance of passing down knowledge and expertise.
Mentees are matched with the right mentors.	Mentees may be asked to consider their mentoring objectives before matching takes place. Mentors may be asked to list their areas of expertise/experience (can also be from a predetermined list).
Parties are briefed.	Either one-to-one or small group briefing sessions to help candidates understand the role of a good mentor and mentee. Short briefing packs may be provided for all mentors and mentees as a reminder of their role and what is important (including advice for the first meeting).
Informal follow-up.	Formal set up and matching process but light touch once relationships are set up.
Monitoring.	This may be as detailed or as necessary for internal purposes. However, regular 'informal' check-ins with mentors and mentees by someone responsible for the programme are important to success.

FIGURE 8.6

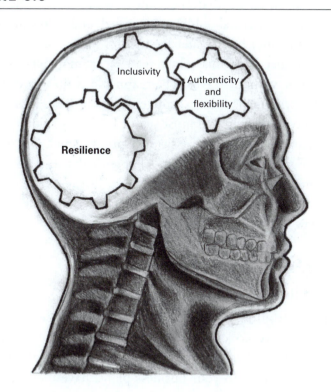

Resilience

Identifying and managing Executive Gremlins build resilience and we have focused a lot on this in earlier chapters in this book. I have described in detail why we need to worry about this and how we can go about it. As we discovered in the last chapter, the rot starts at the top. Organizations must first build a resilient board that reflects the needs and aspirations of the business. Executives are often under huge amounts of pressure and they must be able to handle whatever is thrown at them without caving in under the pressure. Non-executive directors should have relevant industry experience and contacts but also have been through enough crucibles of experience to add value in times of crisis. Aspiring talent should be trained to handle the pressure so that they know what to do when it hits them. Critical players should be identified and allowances made for down time after a particularly stressful time. The armed forces recognize the need for this. Their leaders are not expected to do tour after tour without leave. Yet organizations do expect this and are often surprised when top executives burn out. There is still stigma attached to seeking help and most senior leaders wouldn't dream of contacting an EAP (employee assistance programme). Organizations can feel like war zones. We saw in Chapter 5 that the brain cannot tell the difference between fact and fiction. If leaders are constantly experiencing overload and threat responses, they will eventually break down.

Practical steps

Step 1: Build a resilient board

Look at composition, individual value and resilience. If necessary, provide executive coaching to support them. Assess your non-executive directors and identify what value they are adding. Do they really add value to your business plans, have they 'been there' and do they have networks of relevant contacts in the countries you seek to operate that can help you succeed or are they adding to a comfortable portfolio career and delivering little?

Step 2: Build a resilient culture

Hold regular offsites to encourage thinking about culture and growth as well as just current figures and performance. Give leaders permission to admit that they are struggling before they burn out. Allow project down time between periods of intense pressure as a normal part of the leadership role and allow them back if they need time out.

Step 3: Train every leader in how to manage stress in themselves and their teams

Make The Executive Advantage 10-Step Solution and neuroleadership training available to all and build it into existing leadership programmes from graduate to executive.

Step 4: Provide executive coaching and mentoring to critical players who may be at risk of burnout

Ensure that the coaches chosen are adept at coaching around stress. The coaching industry has been at pains to separate from counselling and therapy and they are distinct fields. However, there are times when an experienced coach has a unique opportunity to help someone through a particularly challenging time. When I interviewed clients for my doctorate, they helped me identify that my original contribution to knowledge lay in my ability to help them unravel a complicated stressful situation. There is a therapeutic element to this and the government has described 'any intervention that seeks to change behaviour' as therapeutic. Many executives are not comfortable seeking therapy but will share with a suitably qualified coach or mentor. Burnout may be averted.

Resilience is the key to enabling the other two capabilities for 21st-century leadership. Without it leaders will not be able to be authentically flexible and agile, or inclusive.

The Executive Advantage for Resilient 21st-century Leadership programme includes the following objectives:

- to recognize the importance of Executive Gremlins in the derailment of business strategy;
- to understand the pressures of 21st-century leadership and the core capabilities required to handle them, including authentic flexibility and agility, inclusive leadership and resilience;
- to manage Executive Gremlins more effectively using The Executive Advantage 10-Step Solution for Resilient 21st-century Leaders©;
- to handle conflict and politics and improve influencing skills at all levels;
- to explore personal leadership styles and how to be authentic role models and mentors (including neuroleadership);
- to encourage cognitive diversity and metacognition – to think about their thinking.

The programme is not about specific skills development, training or curriculum-based teaching. It is not psychotherapy. It is based on leading-edge principles applied in top-level executive coaching and authentic leadership. Actions and takeaways are encouraged but are not prescribed. Learning is not restricted to the sessions themselves but takes place as participants experience new situations and insights they can take back into their day jobs. It is not a place to be a passive recipient.

The programme is a powerful leadership intervention focused on senior executives and top talent in businesses. It is reliant on you taking ownership and action. It is a programme with strong foundations of *self*-awareness, reflection and self-realization. It is reliant on you to demonstrate leadership behaviours and to make effective decisions; it is an aid to superior behaviours and performance and provides support through facilitation and injection of best practice.

Conclusions and summary

"*Companies can go from obscurity to an estimated $100 billion market cap (Facebook) or from zero to $1 billion in revenue (Groupon) very quickly, or from near collapse in the late 90s to become one of the world's most valuable companies (Apple). To succeed today, companies need to embrace change.*

HARVARD LAW SCHOOL FORUM ON CORPORATE GOVERNANCE AND FINANCIAL REGULATION, JUNE 2012

The key proposition in this book is that resilience is vital to 21st-century leadership and that Executive Gremlins cause poor decision making in leaders which ultimately contribute to, or may even cause, business derailment.

The concerns of 21st-century leaders at the top of organizations are to manage change and complexity in an increasingly globalized world of unstable markets, talent shortages, rising energy costs, population explosion in the East, new technology and the emerging of new world superpowers (China and India). These issues bring with them new challenges, demands and pressures including pace, change, complexity, globalization of markets and 24/7 culture. Constant travel, video conferencing and the increased speed of all types of communication, and downsizing (doing more with less) have also taken their toll. All of this affects businesses even when they are not global. Today's businesses have to be agile, networked and innovative. Thus, leaders are under unprecedented levels of stress. The solutions offered in this book focus on two areas – *solutions for individual business leaders* (The Executive Advantage 10-Step Solution for 21st-century Leaders©) and *solutions for organizations* (steps and solutions for each core leadership capability, top tips for CEOs, and mentoring programmes).

Twenty-first-century organizations need leaders with capabilities to address the challenges above in the following areas:

- *Resilience* (the main focus of this book, including the 10-Step Solution in Chapter 4);
- *Authentic flexibility and agility* (which cannot be achieved without resilience);
- *Inclusivity* (to reflect organizations' employee and customer base).

Twenty-first-century leaders need solutions to the relentless pressure, which I have provided in the 10-Step Solution for Resilient 21st-century Leaders© and neuroleadership solutions.

In this book we looked at:

- *Resilience under fire* – organizational situations that cause Executive Gremlins, including aggressive growth, MBOs and flotations, joint ventures and downsizing.
- *The secret weapon* – knowing what your Executive Gremlins are and recognizing those of others by exploring three core executive needs (to feel important, to be popular, and to be in control) and some supporting ones, like the need to feel good enough, powerful, strong and intelligent (reflecting the Executive Gremlins of Unimportant, Unlovable, Out of control, Not good enough, Powerless, Weak and Stupid!).
- *Your reality is not their reality* – how our perceptions form filters through which we see the world. These perceptions are based on patterns that exist in our minds, which come about as a result of positive and negative experiences from our past. These form 'areas of sensitivity' or Executive Gremlins, limiting self-beliefs that we have about ourselves that cause

us to make poor decisions and in extreme circumstances to derail. The derailment of business leaders inevitably leads to poor business performance of the organization.

- *The 10-Step Solution for Resilient 21st-century Leaders*© and saw how the process works with leaders in organizations.

- *Neuroleadership* and how my 10-Step Solution fits. We explored how humans perceive the world initially as friend or foe and register either a threat or a reward response. We discovered that when we perceive a threat, our prefrontal cortex, responsible for rational thought, shuts down and the amygdala, part of the limbic system, reacts – our animal brain takes over and we attack. We also learned that the brain does not know the difference between physical danger and emotional threats.

- *Women on the edge* explored how Executive Advantage applies to women specifically. I provided top tips for CEOs for getting more women on boards.

- *The rot starts at the top* and reviewed how top leaders must make the shift first if they are to transition their organizations to 21st-century cultures and overcome the challenges faced. The biggest reason for long-term sick leave at all levels of organizations today is stress. Leaders are not immune. Organizations need to change their approach if they are to transition their cultures. The 10-Step Solution for Resilient 21st-century Leaders© and the solutions provided for organizations will address these issues. If leaders can self-regulate in the moment, they will be able to make better decisions.

- *The Executive Advantage Solution for 21st-century Organizations.* If leaders of organizations really want to transition their organizations to face the challenges ahead they must put in place new organizational development solutions to old organizational problems that are becoming more pressing (inclusivity, authentic flexibility and agility and resilience). We looked at how thought leadership, development and mentoring programmes can help.

21st-century leaders today must consider multiple stakeholders and a fragmented job, matching their leadership style to fast-paced complex businesses. They must hold multiple perspectives without being overloaded and be able to manage their Executive Gremlins and recognize stress in others. They must work with people in virtual teams, often communicating by video conferencing, and be aware of unconscious bias in themselves and others. They must create a compelling vision and align people to it, overcoming disputes to achieve business goals. They can no longer control the environment – they must empower and delegate instead. The current state of global markets makes it imperative that all this is done within a framework of cutting overheads short term whilst building long-term business. Finally, they must collaborate with all stakeholders – customers, suppliers, competitors and internally.

Paul Polman (CEO of Unilever) said 'I don't work for the shareholder, I work for consumers and my customers.'

Successful 21st-century leaders focus on sustaining superior performance by aligning people around mission and values and empowering leaders at all levels, whilst concentrating on serving customers and collaborating internally. This was an approach taken by Sam Palmisano, when he joined IBM, who developed an 'integrated global network', shifting the leadership approach to 'leading by values'.

The Executive Advantage leadership programme, or at least a module teaching leaders and top talent the 10-Step Solution for Resilient 21st-century Leaders, should be on every business school and organizational leadership development curriculum.

The Executive Advantage 10-Step Solution for Resilient 21st-century Leaders© *works*. It is detailed in full in Chapter 4, and if you have read this book and worked through the process, and if you persevere with it over a period of time, you will create new neural pathways in your brain, more helpful beliefs and will learn to manage your Executive Gremlins. This will in turn help you to make better decisions *in the moment* when facing difficult organizational issues. If you wish to learn how to do this with others you will need training. The Executive Advantage Solution for 21st-century Organizations© works too. These solutions work with and improve other stress management solutions. The responsibility for change lies with governments, with organizations, and, ultimately, with you.

Further reading

George, B (2003) *Authentic Leadership: Rediscovering the Secrets to Creating Lasting Value*, Jossey Bass, San Francisco, CA

Kets de Vries, M L (2006) *The Leader on the Couch*, John Wiley and Sons, Chichester

Maitland, A and Wittenberg-Cox (2008) *Why Women Mean Business*, John Wiley and Sons, Chichester

Maitland, A and Thomson, P (2011) *Future Work*, Palgrave Macmillan, Basingstoke

Oncken, W and Wass, D L (1999) Management time: who's got the monkey? *Harvard Business Review*, 77 (6), pp 178–80

Rock, D and Schwartz, J (2006) The neuroscience of leadership, *Strategy and Business Magazine*, **43**, pp 2–10

Rock, D (2007) *Quiet Leadership*, HarperCollins, New York

Rock, D (2008) A brain-based model for collaborating with and influencing others, *The Neuroleadership Journal*, **1** (1), pp 44–52

Rock, D (2009) *Your Brain at Work*, HarperCollins, New York

Action

Contact Jacqui at Transition Ltd to discuss Executive Advantage 21st-century solutions for leaders and organizations:
www.transition-coaching.co.uk
Tel 01344 625966

BIBLIOGRAPHY

Abbs, P (2003) *Against The Flow – Education, the arts and postmodern culture*, Routledge Falmer, London

Arkowitz, H (1997) cited in Corey, G (2001) Article 29: Designing an integrative approach to counselling practice, *Vistas Online*, **10**(2), pp 271–91

Aristotle, translated by M Pakaluk (1998) *Nichomachean Ethics*, Oxford University Press, USA

Batstone, D (2003) *Saving the Corporate Soul – and (Who Knows?) Maybe Your Own*, Jossey-Bass, San Francisco, CA

Beaches (1988) Film. Directed by G Marshall, Touchstone Pictures, Los Angeles

Bennis, W A T, Robert, J (2002) *Geeks and Geezers – How era, values and defining moments shape leaders*, Harvard Business School Press, Boston, MA

Benton, D A (2005) *Executive Charisma – 6 Steps to Mastering the Art of Leadership*, McGraw-Hill, Maidenhead

Black, J (1994) *MindStore – The Ultimate Mental Fitness Programme*, Thorsons/Element, London

Blackburn, S (2005) *Oxford Dictionary of Philosophy*, Oxford University Press, Oxford

Blanchard, K, Oncken Jr, W, Burrows, H (1989) *The One Minute Manager Meets the Monkey*, Quill William Morrow, New York

Bosq, M (2002) *The Inner Warrior*, Writers Club Press, Bloomington, IN

Bowles, P (1998) *The Sheltering Sky*, HarperCollins, UK

Bradley, R T (1987) *Charisma and Social Structure – A Study of Love and Power, Wholeness and Transformation*, iUniverse

Braiker, H B (2004) *Who's Pulling Your Strings – How to Break the Cycle of Manipulation and Regain Control of Your Life*, McGraw-Hill, Maidenhead

Briggs, I and Myers, P (1980, 1995) *Gifts Differing: Understanding Personality Type*, Davies-Black Publishing, Mountain View, CA

Brodkey, L (1987) Writing ethnographic narratives, *Sage Journals*, **4** (1), pp 25–50

Burnett, M (2005–2007) *The Apprentice (UK)*, TV Programme, BBC, United Kingdom

Camus, A (1955) *The Myth of Sisyphus*, Knopf, New York

Carnap, R (1950) *Logical Foundations of Probability*, University of Chicago Press, Chicago

Carter, K and Pelphrey, E (2008) Charting the typical and atypical development of the social brain, *Development and Psychopathology*, **20**, pp 1081–102 doi:10.1017/S0954579408000515

Chagani, F (1998) Postmodernism – rearranging the furniture of the universe, *Irreverence*, **1** (3), pp 1–3

Checkland, P (1981) cited in Gill, J and Johnson, P (2002) *Research Methods for Managers*, Sage Publications Limited, London, p9

Clutterbuck, P D (2005) *The Seven Layers of Mentoring*, [Online] http://www.gptrainingconsultants.com/tools-and-resources

Coates, J M and Herbert, J (2008) Endogenous steroids and financial risk taking on a London trading floor, *Proceedings of the National Academy of Sciences of the United States of America*, **105** (16), pp 6167–72

Corey, G (2001) Article 29: Designing an integrative approach to counselling practice, *Vistas Online*, **10**(2), pp 271–91

Covey, S A I (2002) *Leadership and Self Deception – Getting out of the box*, Berrett-Koehler Publishers, Inc., San Francisco, CA

Damon, W (2004) *The Moral Advantage – How to Succeed in Business by Doing the Right Thing*, Berrett-Koehler Publishers, Inc., San Francisco, CA

Denning, S (2000) *The Springboard*, Butterworth-Heinemann, Cambridge, MA

Dickson, A (2006) *Difficult Conversations. What to Say in Tricky Situations Without Ruining the Relationship*, Piatkus Books Limited, London

Dostoyevsky, F (2003) *The Brothers Karamazov*, Penguin Books, London

Dostoyevsky, F (2004) *Notes from the Underground*, Everyman's Library, London

Douglas, B and Moustakas, C (1985) Heuristic inquiry: the internal search to know, *Journal of Humanistic Psychology*, **25**, p 50

Downfall (2004) Film. Directed by O Hirschbiegel, Newmarket Capital Group, Los Angeles, CA

Eisenberger, N and Lieberman, M (2009) The pains and pleasures of social life: a social cognitive neuroscience approach, *Science*, **323** (5916), pp 890–91

Elkad-Lehman, I (2005) Spinning a tale: intertextuality and intertextual aptitude, *L1-Educational Studies in Language and Literature*, **5**(1), pp 39–56

Ellis, D (2002) *Falling Awake – Creating the Life of Your Dreams*, Breakthrough Enterprises, Inc., New York

Flanders, M (1994) *Breakthrough – The Career Woman's Guide to Shattering the Glass Ceiling*, Paul Chapman Publishing, London

Fontana, D (2001) *Discover Zen – A Practical Guide to Personal Serenity*, Chronicle Books, San Francisco, CA

Forster, M (2006) *Do It Tomorrow And Other Secrets of Time Management*, Bookmarque Ltd, Hodder & Stoughton, London

Frankl, V (1946) *Man's Search for Meaning*, Beacon Press, Boston MA

Gardner, W L, Bruce, J, *et al* (2005) *Authentic Leadership – theory and practice – Origins, Effects and Development*, Elsevier, Oxford

Garratt, B (1996) *The Fish Rots from the Head – The Crisis in Our Boardrooms: Developing the Crucial Skills of the Competent Director*, HarperCollins Business, New York

George, B (2003) *Authentic Leadership – Rediscovering the Secrets of Creating Lasting Value*, Jossey-Bass, San Francisco, CA

George, B (2007) *True North: Discover Your Authentic Leadership*, Jossey-Bass, San Francisco, CA

Gill, J and Johnson, P (2002) *Research Methods for Managers*, Sage Publications Limited, London

Goffee, R and Jones, G (2006) *Why Should Anyone Be Led by You?: What It Takes To Be An Authentic Leader*, Harvard Business School Press, Boston, MA

Goleman, D (1999) *Working with Emotional Intelligence*, Bloomsbury Publishing, London

Goleman, D (2002) *The New Leaders – Emotional Intelligence at Work*, Little, Brown, London

Gordon, E (2000) *Integrative Neuroscience: Bringing Together Biological, Psychological and Clinical Models of the Human Brain*, CRC Press, USA

Grant, A M (2003) Keeping up with the Cheese! Research as a foundation for professional coaching of the future, *1st ICP Coaching Research Symposium*, International Coach Federation, Denver, Colorado

Gray, D E (2006) Executive coaching: towards a dynamic alliance of psychotherapy and transformative learning processes, *Management Learning*, 37 (4), pp 475–497

Gur, R C and Gur, R E (2004) Gender differences in the functional organization of the brain, in M J Legato (ed) *Principles of Gender-specific Medicine* (pp 63–70), Elsevier, Amsterdam

Hall, L (2006) A whole new ballpark, *Coaching at Work Magazine*, July 7, pp 40–41

Hall, M P (1959) *Basic Fears And How to Correct Them – Lectures on Personal Growth*, The Philosophical Research Society, Inc., Los Angeles, CA

Handy, C (1998) *The Hungry Spirit: Beyond Capitalism – A Quest for Purpose in the Modern World*, Broadway, Blackpool

Handy, C (2006) *Myself and Other More Important Matters*, Heinemann

Handy, C (2006) *The New Philanthropists: The New Generosity*, Heinemann, London

Handy, C (2007) A very handy philosophy, *Business Strategy Review*, **18**(1), pp 5–10

Haslam, S A and Ryan, M K (2005) The glass cliff: evidence that women are over-represented in precarious leadership positions, *British Journal of Management*, **16** (2), pp 81–90

Hedden, T and Gabrieli, J D E (2006) The ebb and flow of attention in the human brain, *Nature Neuroscience*, **9**, pp 863–65

Heidegger, M (1962) *Being and Time*, Harper, San Francisco, CA

Hobbs, C L (2005) *The Elements of Autobiography and Life Narratives*, Pearson Education, Inc., London

Huczynski, A (1993) *Management Gurus – What Makes Them and How to Become One*, Routledge Publishing, London

Human Givens Institute [accessed 18 October 2012] The human givens approach, *The Human Givens Institute* [Online] www.hgi.org.uk

Ibarra, H (2004) *Working Identity: Unconventional Strategies for Reinventing Your Career*, Harvard Business School Press, Boston, MA

ICF (2003) *A Model of Excellence: Annual International Conference*, Montreal, Canada

Idzikowski, C (2000) *Learn to Sleep Well*, Duncan Baird Publishers, London

Jacobs, G D (2001) The physiology of mind–body interactions: the stress response and the relaxation response, *The Journal of Alternative and Complementary Medicine*, **7** (supplement 1), pp 83–92, doi:10.1089/107555301753393841

Janov, A (1973) *Primal Scream*, Abacus, London

Janov, A (1993) *The New Primal Scream – Primal Therapy Twenty Years On*, Abacus, London

Jeffers, S (1996) *End The Struggle and Dance With Life – How to Build Yourself Up When The World Gets You Down*, Coronet Books, Philadelphia, PA

Jeffers, S (1987) *Feel the Fear and Do It Anyway*, Hodder & Stoughton, London

Jung, C (1971) *The Collected Works of C.G. Jung*, Princeton University Press, Princeton, NJ

Kampa-Kokesch, S (2001) Executive coaching – A comprehensive review of the literature, *Consulting Psychology Journal: Practice and Research*, **53**(4), pp 205–28

Keenan, B (1992) *An Evil Cradling*, Hutchinson, London

Kerzner, H (2004) *Advanced Project Management*, John Wiley & Sons, Chichester

Kets de Vries, M and Engellau, E (2004) *Are leaders born or are they made?, The case of Alexander the Great*, Karnac (Books) Ltd, London

Kets de Vries, M F R and Danny, M (1987) *Unstable at the Top – Inside the troubled organisation*, Mentor, New York

Kets de Vries, M and Danny, M (2004) *Are Leaders Born Or Are They Made?* Karnac (Books) Ltd, London

Kets de Vries, M F R (1984) *The Irrational Executive, Psychoanalytic Explorations in Management*, International Universities Press, Madison, CT

Kets de Vries, M F R (1989) *Prisoners of Leadership*, John Wiley & Sons, Chichester

Kets de Vries, M F R (1995) *Life and Death in the Executive Fast Lane*, Jossey-Bass, San Francisco, CA

Kets de Vries, M F R (2003) *Leaders, Fools and Impostors: Essays on the Psychology of Leadership*, iUniverse

Kets de Vries, M F R (2006) *The Leader on the Couch – A clinical approach to changing people and organizations*, Jossey-Bass, San Francisco, CA

Kierkegaard, S (1986) *Fear and Trembling*, Cambridge University Press, Cambridge

Kilburg (2000) cited in Kampa-Kokesch, S (2001) Executive coaching – A comprehensive review of the literature, *Consulting Psychology Journal: Practice and Research*, 53(4), pp 205–28

King, M F (2005) *Inner Fears*, Coscom Entertainment, Canada

Kogan Page (2005) *A letter from potential publishers*, Kogan Page, London

Kozubska, J (1997) *The 7 Keys of Charisma – Unlocking the secrets of those who have it*, Kogan Page, London

Laslett, B (2004) Biography as historical sociology, *Theory and Sociotype*, 20(4), pp 511–38

Leiberman, D J (2006) *How to Change Anybody*, St Martin's Griffin, New York

Loureiro, A G (2000) *The Ethics of Autobiography*, Vanderbilt University Press

Lowndes, L (2003) *How to Talk to Anyone – 92 Little Tricks for Big Success in Relationships*, McGraw-Hill, Maidenhead

Made in Dagenham (2010) Film. Directed by Nigel Cole, BBC Films, London

Maitland, A and Wittenberg-Cox, A (2008) *Why Women Mean Business*, John Wiley & Sons, Chichester

Marino, G (2004) *Basic Writings of Existentialism*, Modern Library, New York

Marsh, S (2007) Losing it, *The Times*, 2 August

Martin, R (2002) *The Responsibility Virus: How Control Freaks, Shrinking Violets – and the Rest of Us – can Harness the Power of True Partnership*, Basic Books, New York

Martindale, J and Mary, J (1999) *No More Bag Lady Fears – A Woman's Guide to Retirement Planning*, Writers Club Press, Bloomington, IN

Maslow (1956) *Self actualising people*, Harper and Brothers, New York

McGinnis, D A L (2004) *The Friendship Factor: How to get closer to the people you care for*, Augsburg Fortress, Minneapolis, MN

Megginson, D and Clutterbuck, D (1995) *Mentoring in Action*, Kogan Page, London

Miles, N (2008) *The double-glazed glass ceiling: lesbians in the workplace* [Report] Stonewall, London

Moir, A and Jessel, D (1992) *Brainsex: The Real Difference Between Men and Women*, Dell Publishing, New York

Mommie Dearest (1981) Film. Directed by P Fred, Paramount Pictures, Los Angeles, CA

Moustakas, C (1990) *Heuristic Research*, Sage Publications, London

Mumford, A (1990) *Developing Top Managers*, Gower Publishing, Farnham, Surrey

Nietzsche, F (2003) *Beyond Good and Evil*, Penguin Classics, London

Oncken Jr, W and Wass, D (1986) *Who's Got the Monkey?* Prentice Hall, New Jersey, USA

Parkhouse, S (2001) *Powerful Women Dancing on the Glass Ceiling*, John Wiley & Sons, Chichester

Pauchant, T C, Morin, E M and Morin, P E M (2006) Organizational existentialism, *International Encyclopedia of Organizational Studies*, (ed) S Clegg, Sage Publications, Thousand Oaks, CA

Pellegrinelli, S and David, P (2006) Pitfalls in taking a project-based view of programmes, *PMI Global Congress Proceedings*, Madrid, Spain

Peltier, B (2001) *The Psychology of Executive Coaching – Theory and Application*, Brunner-Routledge, Hove, East Sussex

Peters, T (1997) *In Search of Excellence: Lessons from America's Best Run Companies*, G K Hall & Co., Boston, MA

Philadelphia (1993) Film. Directed by J Demme, TriStar Pictures, Los Angeles, CA

Polanyi, M (1969) *Knowing and Being: Essays by Michael Polanyi*, University of Chicago Press, Chicago, IL

Polanyi, M (1983) *The Tacit Dimension*, Peter Smith Publisher Inc, Gloucester, MA

Reeb, L (2005) *From Success to Significance*, OMF Literature Inc, Manila, Philippines

Reynolds, J (2006) *Understanding Existentialists*, Acumen Publications, Chesham

Riviere, J (1952) The unconscious phantasy (sic) of an inner world reflected in English Literature, *The International Journal of Psychoanalysis*, **33**, pp 160–72

Rock, D (2002) *Intensive Coach Training*, Results Coaching Systems, India

Rock, D (2008) SCARF: A brain-based model for collaborating with and influencing others, *Neuroleadership Journal*, **1** (1), pp 44–52

Rock, D and Schwartz, J [accessed 18 October 2012] The neuroscience of leadership, *Strategy and Business* [Online] www.strategy-business.com/press/article/06207

Rogers, J (2006) *Coaching Skills – A Handbook*, Open University Press, London

Rorty, R (2003) *A Pragmatist View of Contemporary Analytic Philosophy – The Pragmatic Turn in Philosophy*, SUNY Press, New York

Roskind, R (1992) *In the Spirit of Business – A Guide to Resolving Fears and Creating Harmony in the Worklife*, Celestial Arts, Berkeley, CA

Rowe, D (2007) Which comes first, the job or the depression? *The Times*, August

Rudestam, K E and Newton, R R (2001) *Surviving Your Dissertation: A Comprehensive Guide to Content and Process*, Sage Publications, Thousand Oaks, CA

Sapolski, R (2002) *Why Zebras Don't Get Ulcers*, Henry Holt and Company, USA

Sartre, J P (1943) *Being and Nothingness* cited in Marino, G (2004) *Basic Writings on Existentialism*, Modern Library Classics, London

Sartre, J P (1957) *Existentialism and Human Emotions*, Citadel Press, New York

Schultz, W (1979) *Profound Simplicity*, Joy Press, London

Schultz, W (1999) The reward signal of midbrain dopamine neurons, *Physiology*, **14** (6), pp 249–55

Scratchpad, W [accessed 31 October 2012] The Art of Explication [Online] http://scratchpad.wikia.com/wiki/Art_of_explication

Seamark, M (2011) Lloyds boss goes sick with 'stress': shock departure eight months into job, *Daily Mail*, 3 November

Shapiro, G (2011) *Opportunity Now: Inclusive Leadership – from Pioneer to Mainstream: Maximizing the Potential of your People*, Business in the Community, London

Sieler, A (2003) *Coaching to the Human Soul: ontological coaching and deep change*, Blackburn, Victoria

Singer *et al* (2006) Empathic neural responses are modulated by the perceived fairness of others, *Nature*, **439**, 466–69

Sperry (1996) cited in Spigelman, C (2004) *Personally Speaking: Experience as evidence in academic discourse*, Southern Illinois University Press, Carbondale IL

Spinelli, E (2001) *The Mirror and The Hammer – Challenges to Therapeutic Orthodoxy*, Sage Publications, Thousand Oaks, CA

Spinelli, E (2005) *The Interpreted World: An introduction to phenomenological psychology*, Sage Publications, Thousand Oaks, CA

Spinelli, E and Horner, C (2006) Life's rich tapestry, *Coaching at Work*, 1 November 2006, pp 42–43

Spinelli, P E (2007) *An Existential Approach to Coaching*, Ernesto Spinelli and Associates, Boston, MA

Stoker, B (2006) *Positive Risk – How Smart Women use Passion to Break Through their Fears*, Jossey-Bass, San Francisco, CA

Strasser, F (1999) *Emotions – Experiences in Existential Psychotherapy and Life*, Duckworth, London

Tabibnia, G and Lieberman, M D (2007) Fairness and cooperation are rewarding: evidence from social cognitive neuroscience, *Annals of the New York Academy of Sciences*, **1118**, pp 90–101

Taylor, D (2002) *The Naked Leader*, Capstone Publishing, Mankato, MN

Tincher, J (2001, 2002) Discover the wealth within you, *Weekender*, **4**

Trainspotting (1996) Film. Directed by Danny Boyle, Channel Four Films, London

Turner, A (2006) Preface (to my dissertation), *A better description of leadership coaching* [Unpublished]

Valerio, A M and Lee, R J (2004) *Executive Coaching: A Guide for the HR Professional*, Pfeiffer, San Francisco, CA

Van der Horst, B (2008) The law of requisite contrariety, practical paradoxes to live by, and other notes on the illusion of failure, *Integral Leader Review*, August

Vasella D (2003) cited in George (2003)

Weick, K E (1995) *Sensemaking in Organisations*, Sage, London

Welch, J (2005) *Winning*, HarperCollins, New York

Whitmore, S J (2006) Driving Force, *Coaching at Work*, **37**, pp 38–39

Whitmore, S J (1996) *Coaching for Performance*, Nicholas Brealey Publishing, London

Whitworth, L, Kimsey-House, H and Sandahl, P (1998) *Co-Active Coaching*, Davies-Black Publishing, Mountain View, CA

Williamson, M (1996) *A Return to Love: Reflections on the Principles of 'A Course in Miracles'*, HarperCollins, New York

Wirth, L (2001) *Breaking Through The Glass Ceiling: Women in Management*, International Labour Office, Switzerland

Zander, R S and Zander, B (2000) *The Art of Possibility: Transforming Professional and Personal Life*, Harvard Business School Press, Boston, MA

Zeus, P and Suzanne, S (2001) *The Complete Guide to Coaching at Work*, McGraw-Hill, Maidenhead

Zwick, C C (2000) *Fourteen Tales to Take You to Places You've Never Been*, Xlibris Corporation, Bloomington, IN

INDEX

(italics indicate a figure or table in the text)